KESWICK SE

Keswick Seventysix

Edited by
J. Hywel-Davies

COVERDALE HOUSE PUBLISHERS
LONDON AND EASTBOURNE

© 1976 Keswick Convention Council

ISBN 0 902088 86 6

All rights reserved.
No part of this book may be used or reproduced
in any manner whatsoever without written
permission from the publishers, except in the case
of brief quotations embodied in critical articles
and reviews.

Black and white photographs by Canon K. W. Coates

Cover photographs:
  Outside views by Charles Henshall
  Tent interior by Don Feltham

Printed in Great Britain for Coverdale House Publishers Ltd.,
Lottbridge Drove, Eastbourne, East Sussex, BN23 6NT
by Hunt Barnard Printing Ltd., Aylesbury, Bucks.

CONTENTS

Foreword: The Revd. Canon A. S. Neech   9

Impressions: Dr. J. Hywel-Davies   11

Bible Readings – First Week:
   The Revd. Eric J. Alexander

   The Fellowship of Light and Love –
     Four Studies in the First Epistle of John

   Part 1. The Message and its Implications   15
   Part 2. The Evidence of Walking in the Light   28
   Part 3. The Privileges and Obligations of being
          children of God   42
   Part 4. The Implications of Abiding in Love
          Conclusion: The Full Assurance of
          Faith   56

Bible Readings – Second Week:
   The Revd. J. Alec Motyer

Contents

A Single, Steady Aim –
Four Studies in the Book of Nehemiah

Part 1.	Beginning: Getting the Foundations right	69
Part 2.	Persevering: Stress-points and Strong-points	80
Part 3.	Living: (a) The Citizen's Charter	91
Part 4.	Living: (b) The Enemy Within	101

Additional contributors – First and Second Weeks

The Revd. Eric J. Alexander	113
The Revd. Gordon Bridger	118
The Revd. Michael Cole	126
The Revd. George B. Duncan	131, 137
The Revd. Tom Houston	143, 149
The Revd. Gilbert W. Kirby	159, 163
Mr. Alan Nute	169
The Revd. G. Osei-Mensah	174, 180
The Revd. Derek Prime	184
The Revd. Dr. Alan Redpath	189, 196, 202
The Revd. Canon Harry Sutton	208, 218, 225, 233
The Revd. Dr. Skevington Wood	241, 245

Index of Tape Recordings   254

KESWICK SEVENTYSIX

FOREWORD

*by the Revd. Canon Alan S. Neech, L.Th.
(Chairman of the Keswick Convention)*

No written record can possibly recapture the atmosphere of the Keswick Convention. It needs a personal visit to experience the inspiration of being with fellow Christians from every corner of the British Isles, and many other countries, as they give rapt attention to the hearing of God's Word. This year nationals or missionaries came from fifty-eight different countries. Many came from lonely places, having had little or no fellowship with other Christians through the year. What a thrill to sit for a whole hour's exposition of the First Epistle of John each morning of the first week, or of Nehemiah in the second! The sound of rustling pages as Bibles were opened, and references checked, is something that recordings do not pick up, but are one of the memories of those who shared in these great gatherings.

So many different parts together make up the whole Keswick experience. The full throated singing of the now familiar modern hymns in KESWICK PRAISE. The silent dignity of the two great Communion services. The crowds on their way to the early morning prayer meetings. The witness in the market square. The creaking ropes and flapping canvas as the big tent strains in the wind. And the quiet beauty of the hills and lake with the five flags fluttering from the fifty-five feet high tent-poles – all this and much, much more will come to mind as many pick up this book.

But Keswick is not merely a collection of experiences like these, delightful as they are. Each of the two weeks provides an intensive course of teaching in the great Scriptural truths about man's deep need and God's provision in Christ through his Holy Spirit. The Convention ministry provides faithful, honest, careful, scholarly, relevant exegesis of the Word of God through the lips of some of the world's leading evangelical preachers and Bible teachers. Every year thousands learn again what Jeremiah meant when he wrote, 'Thy words were found and I did eat them and thy word was unto me the joy and rejoicing of my heart.'

KESWICK SEVENTYSIX is not a verbatim report of all that was said at Keswick. Such reports are far too expensive to produce, especially when tape recordings of all the addresses are available through the Convention's tape ministry. Here, with great skilfulness and using the actual words of the speaker in an abridged form, Dr. J. Hywel-Davies has given us a very readable record of all the main addresses.

Now it goes out and all around the world will be read with much appreciation. Some of it may help in sermon preparation in many other tongues. That has happened before! Pass it on when you have read it. Better still give a copy to a friend who is serving the Lord. Like the Word of God itself this too will be 'seed for the sower and bread for the eater'.

IMPRESSIONS OF KESWICK SEVENTYSIX

by the Editor

'Perhaps we should ask *Elisha* Buckley to do the same thing for us in reverse.' And the crowd laughed. Eric Alexander's comment on the rain falling on the Keswick Convention tent, the first break in the unusually dry sunny season in the lake district, and Tim Buckley's passionate prayer of the previous day for clouds of rain. This was Keswick in its relaxed happy mood ready to sit back and listen to one of the ablest and most interesting speakers I have heard in my lifetime. And within the limits of the editorial space at my disposal I hope I will have done justice to him. For the asides and the anecdotes, such as the one above, you should buy one of the excellent recordings of Helmut Kaufmann listed on pages 254 and 255.

Rain after sunshine is cleansing and refreshing. And that sums up *Keswick Seventysix* for me. This is not a report. Just a collection of impressions. And the overall one is of deep Bible teaching coupled with an inspirational challenge generously sprinkled with human humour. I emphasize the human part of the humour. It was not contrived, produced from a factory-belt of script-writers. It was born of experience. Harry Sutton recounting how he met his wife as an answer to a young convert's prayer from the pulpit of St. John's Keswick, to illustrate a point in his sermon, is something I shall never forget. Regretfully, there were no recording facilities for that occasion. The best I can do is to recommend that you plan to visit Keswick next year – even if Harry Sutton isn't there.

My friends, and enemies, will tell you that I am not a natural enthusiast for 'holy huddles'. But the natural atmosphere of this year's Keswick put me at ease from the first second. Not just the spontaneous remarks and the humour to lighten some heavy discourse on a serious subject, but the obviously genuine expressions of love between people in the streets as well as the tents. You could tell who were the Christians in the holiday town even if you were deaf. And in the tent the rapport between the platform and the people would have been the envy of any professional entertainer present. But the speakers didn't pull their punches. There were penetrating questions. Tom Houston demolished a few petty ideas about separatism in his talk on liberation. George Duncan, the softly spoken Scottish 'father', was incisive in his spiritual surgery with his tests of our confessed allegiance to our Lord and Master. Alan Redpath inspired everyone with his call to full commitment and a hunger for the Holy Spirit. And so I could continue. But as the editor I must not take liberties.

This book is the substance of what the speakers said with no words of any consequence added. It can be read quickly or studied closely. I recommend the latter. It's a book to be read with your Bible alongside. Look up the references (the actual words have been omitted in most places in the interests of economy) and follow the speaker through his pattern of thinking. At the end you cannot help being a better man or a better woman.

THE FELLOWSHIP OF LIGHT AND LOVE

Four studies in the First Epistle of John by the Revd. Eric J. Alexander, M.A., B.D.

1. The Message and its Implications

In many ways the first epistle of John is a very unusual New Testament letter. In the second place, it is not addressed to any particular church, although John may have been writing to a group of churches which probably had their centre at Ephesus. In the third place it is significant to note that it is possibly one of the last writings of the New Testament if not the last. Certainly the Apostle John is a very old man as he writes towards the end of the first century A.D. and he is the last survivor of the Apostolic band.

Of the five New Testament books of which we believe John to be the author, the gospel and the first epistle have a close relation to each other in language, style and content. Notice the link between John 20:31 and in 1 John 5:13 where he declares his purpose for these separate writings. In the gospel John says that he has written that 'You might believe that Jesus is the Christ the Son of the living God.' The epistle has a parallel purpose to lead those to whom it is written into full assurance of faith: 'I write this to you who believe that you may know that you have eternal life.'

It seems, however, that that assurance was being attacked, even while John was writing, in the two classical ways in which Christian assurance tends to be attacked. One is an attack on the objective truth of the Gospel (cf. 1 John 2:26). This attack almost certainly came from one of the many heretical groups that we put together under the title of Gnosticism. The belief common to these groups was that physical matter was evil. This meant that they had great difficulty about the Christian teaching concerning the body of Christ, and concerning the body of Christians. They found it difficult to believe that God could take a body, since matter was evil, and they found it difficult to believe that God was concerned about what Christians did with their bodies. The Christian teaching that the body was the temple of the Holy Spirit seemed to them an extraordinary thing. So there was a suspicion of the Christian doctrine of the incarnation of Christ and of the sanctification of believers. Salvation to them was really a process of enlightenment unrelated to ethics or morals. So you find John writing, 'We know him if we keep his commandments.'

But there was another and more subjective attack on the level of doubts about the possession of eternal life, so John instructs them how to reassure their hearts before God (cf. 3:19). John attempts to undergird their personal eternal life. These evidences are, 1. A right obedience to God; 2. A right love for one another; and 3. A right belief of the truth.

The form in which John expounds this teaching is another unique characteristic of the letter making any formal analysis very difficult. The reason for the difficulty is that the course of John's thought does not move

Studies in the First Epistle

from point to point in the way that we find Paul's thought moving. It may be described as symphonic in form. Just as a musical composer will take up one or two themes, developing them, repeating them, inverting their order and combining the whole ultimately into a perfect symphony of sound. Or, to use another metaphor, like a spiral staircase which always recurs to the same area but at a higher level.

In the interests of clarity, I have divided the epistle into two parts, whose themes are, *light and love* (1:5 'God is light'; 4:8 'God is love'). The twofold calling of the Christian therefore, by which his whole Christian standing may be judged, is to 'Walk in the light' (1:7) and to 'Abide in love' (4:16). In a general sense chapters one and two deal with the former, and chapters three to five with the latter.

We begin with *God is light:* THE MESSAGE AND ITS IMPLICATIONS.

Verses one to four of chapter one form a kind of preface or introduction to the whole. They are a foundation on which everything else is built upon. They are also a complement to the prologue of John's gospel (1:1, 14, 15). There is both a similarity and a distinction between the prologue of John and the preface of 1 John. The similarity between the two is this. In both of them, the gospel and the epistle you find the same threefold foundation laid. First, the main theme is of God's eternal *being* and *purpose*. 'In the beginning was the Word and the Word was with God and the Word was God' (John 1:1), and 'That which we have heard and saw, and this we proclaim to you' (1 John 1), is the first parallel.

The second is *historical,* related to God's eternal being. 'The life was made manifest, and we saw it and testified to it' (1:2). The same is expressed in John 1 where he says, 'The Word was made flesh'.

Thirdly, the *personal apprehension* of this revelation. In John's gospel, 'The Word was made flesh and dwelt among us and we beheld his Glory', and in 1 John 1:3, 'That which we have seen and heard we proclaim also to you.' There is also a distinction in the use of the personal *Word*. Whereas in the epistle the emphasis appears to be more on the gospel's revelation. The neuter, 'That which' with which verse one begins, suggests that the emphasis is on the proclamation of the message, as also does the main verb of verses one to three. You will notice that verses one to three are, in many ways, what Professor C. H. Dodds has called 'A grammatical tangle'. But the main verb upon which everything depends does not come until verse three. It is that verb 'We proclaim' on which everything else in this complicated and lengthy sentence hangs. The Apostle's main driving purpose is to emphasise the proclamation, the revelation, rather than the person of Christ. Of course, the two cannot be separated and what ought to be emphasised is that the proclamation is the proclamation of the person of Christ.

From these three verses we see John setting down 1. the foundation of the Christian revelation of God and the gospel which are eternal; 2. its historical setting; and 3. the fact that it was personal and experimental.

Here are a few comments on each of these. This Christian is of a God and a gospel which are eternal in their nature. I understand that to be the meaning of the phrase, 'That which was from the beginning.' This same phrase is used in chapter two, verses thirteen and fourteen regarding God's eternity. In my opinion the

Apostle is speaking about that which was from the beginning in the same sense as he uses the phrase in John's gospel chapter one, and the way it is used in Genesis chapter one. The point is that God's plan and purpose of salvation is like himself, it is eternal (Revelation 14:6). Therefore whenever Christian assurance is under attack, that is the vital doctrine to get hold of. That our salvation is anchored not in any decision of our own nor in anything that belongs merely to the world of time, but in the eternal councils, and in the eternal purpose of an eternal God. We do despite to the doctrines of election and predestination when we use them as a kind of theological hand grenade to throw at each other. They are not given to us for that purpose, they are given as mighty stabilisers.

It is also *historical*. In verse one John writes about all our senses to express the fact that this eternal God has broken into time to work out his eternally conceived plan on the stage of human history. John goes on to state that this gospel is not dealing merely with philosophies, theories or opinions, but with solid facts of verifiable history. This emphasis on the historical is especially necessary in a theological climate where the vogue is to say that whether or not things happened as the New Testament describes them is not the really important thing, that it does not really matter if this history is true, the main thing is the idea that history contains. John says that our faith is rooted in history, our faith is founded on facts of solid verifiable history. We have heard, we have seen, we have touched with our hands the Word of life.

In the third place, neither is it merely a carried story. It is *personal* and experimental (vv. 2, 3). What the Apostle is saying here is that the eternal God has not only broken into history, he has also broken into our lives. Dr. David Smith says, 'There is a gracious constraint on all who know this blessed fellowship, to bring others into it.' The Apostle then goes on to spell out the purpose of his letter in verse three in terms of proclaiming to others what was manifested to them. John Stott says in his commentary, 'The revelation was given to the few for the many.' They were to dispense it to the world. John Bunyan in his preface to *The Jerusalem Sinner Saved,* 'I have been vile myself but have obtained mercy, and would have my companions in sin partake of mercy too, and therefore I have writ this little book.' This is the other John's motive also, 'The message is for the witness and a proclamation and the first of these reasons is that you may have fellowship with us' (vv. 3, 4).

Fellowship in the Biblical, theological sense is a word which includes a reconciliation to God from whose fellowship by sin we are estranged. A continuing relationship with him, in sharing mysteriously, in the fellowship that already exists in content. A. W. Pinkin comments, 'Fellowship is the sum and substance of the whole of true religion.' This is what God has created the world for, fellowship between himself and his creatures. That this is what God has redeemed us for in Christ, fellowship with the Father and the Son. This is what God is preparing us for.

The second great reason is that our joy may be full. The idea is probably a comprehensive one, your joy and our joy. The important thing is that in John's writings in the New Testament fullness of joy can only be found in fellowship with God and in obedience to him. The very fact that we are inclined to seek our joy elsewhere rather than in fellowship with God is evidence that we really need to be persuaded of this that true joy can only be found in God. John Calvin has this beautiful comment, 'Only he has progressed in the Gospel who reckons himself supremely happy in communion with God and rests in that alone.'

There are two things about this message in the phrase, 'God is light, and in him is no darkness at all'. First notice the way that the gospel is defined. 'This is the message we have heard from him, and proclaim to you, that God is Light.' In other words, the Christian gospel is primarily a message about God and it centres upon him (Hebrews 1:1). It begins with God, and with what God is like and with what God has done. The tendency of man's centred thinking is to see the gospel centred upon and beginning with man. We sometimes express this man's centred thinking by expressing the gospel in this way. 'Are you unhappy . . . frustrated . . . facing problems?' 'Come to Jesus and he will deal with them.' Of course, that is perfectly true. He will. But the problem with this man-centred approach is that it makes God man's servant, rather than man God's servant. And the whole order of things is turned upsidedown, and this man-centred emphasis of the gospel produces a self-centred emphasis in Christian living. People imagine that God's great business in the world is to keep them unruffled and happy through the whole of their days, and they suddenly stand back in the midst of a situation and say 'Why is God allowing this to happen to me? This is a gross intrusion into my happiness. I thought God was concerned more about my happiness than anything else.' The Westminster Shorter Catechism is infinitely more Biblical when it says, 'Man's chief end is to glorify God and to enjoy him forever.' The fundamental truth about man has to be seen in the light of that, not in the light of whether I am unhappy at the moment or not.

Secondly, notice the way God is described. 'God is Light and in him is no darkness at all.' Light is a symbol of God for two reasons: first of all, it is the very essence of light that it should shine, and it is the very essence of God that he should reveal himself. That is one of the greatest mysteries of the universe, and it is not because God needs us, God is all-sufficient. But because he is a God of such infinite grace and love he desires to have fellowship with his creatures. However, the second is perhaps the more important sense. When God does reveal himself it is in the character of what light symbolises, absolute holiness and absolute truth. A moral and an intellectual symbolism. By that I mean that light is a symbol of purity and truth, while darkness is a symbol of evil and error. The significance of this is seen in the following passage (1:6 to 2:2). It is that the kind of fellowship we may enjoy with God is determined by his character.

In verses six to ten, John is dealing with three false attitudes to sin and darkness each of them introduced with the phrase, 'If we say' (vv. 6, 8, 10). Each of these is then condemned in a phrase such as 'We lie', 'We deceive ourselves' or 'We make him a liar'. The first false attitude to sin in relationship to fellowship with God (v. 6) is the attitude of libertinism or carelessness about sin, the attitude which says that sin doesn't matter. John's reply to such a claim is comparable to the Apostle Paul's challenge in 2 Corinthians, 6, 'What fellowship has righteousness with unrighteousness . . . ' To the extraordinary claim that some man makes that I am living in fellowship with God while walking in darkness, John makes the stark reply 'You're a liar'.

But what does he mean by walking in the darkness? Basically, it is to follow a course of life which is self-indulging, rather than God-pleasing. Robert Law comments, 'Simply to pursue the everyday life of business and pleasure, of purpose and achievement, without reference to the will of God. To live by the false and mutilated standards of the world. To be blinded by the glare of its artificial illuminations. There are no more effectual and frequented ways than these of "walking in the darkness".' And John says, 'To live like that and to profess to a fellowship with God is to profess a lie.'

In verse seven he turns from the negative to the positive, and it is simply, 'Walking in the light' rather than 'Walking in the darkness'. This means that if walking in the darkness implies tolerating sin, walking in the light would imply turning from sin. It is the very reverse of everything that walking in the darkness means. A twofold result of that is expounded in verse seven. First, we have fellowship one with another. Some people are surprised that John does not go on to say, 'We have fellowship with him'. If walking in the darkness excludes us from fellowship with God, you would have expected the parallel phrase to be, 'If we walk in the light as he is in the light we shall have fellowship with him.' But he doesn't say that. He says, 'We shall have fellowship with one another.' Of course, the one includes the other and the interesting thing is that the fact that we may not realise this, is evidence of how we have devalued true Christian fellowship. Fellowship in the New Testament sense between believers is a total impossibility if they are not separately in fellowship with God by walking in the light.

The other outcome of walking in the light is not only

that we have fellowship with one another, but that the blood of Jesus his Son cleanses us from all sin. To walk in the light is not to be sinless but to bring our sin out into the open before God, and there to discover that he has made provision to deal with everything that would mar our fellowship with him. The tense of the verb implies 'Goes on cleansing'. The point is that the blood of Jesus which first created fellowship between us and God also maintains it.

The second false attitude to sin is introduced in verse eight. If the first wrong attitude is the error of libertinism the second is a form of escapism, or a refusal to accept responsibility for sin. This is an attack upon the whole idea of personal guilt, and this suggestion is made for the very compelling reason that the phrase, 'To have sin' carries with it a definite sense. In John 15:22, for example, the phrase has the same meaning as that of 'Bearing guilt' in John 9:41. This sense would lead naturally into the denial 'We deceive ourselves' and to the correction 'If we confess our sin'. The desire to escape from the responsibility for our sin is a contemporary one. Modern man wants to be treated as an invalid rather than as a sinner. Whereas the Bible states we have no excuse!

Then we need to know what we are saying when we speak about confessing sin. In secular usage, 'To confess' only means to admit. However, the Greek word 'To confess' means 'To say the same things as'. Confession in the Biblical sense is saying the same things as God says about sin. This is most important when we are talking about fellowship with God, because we need to know what we are talking about when we speak of 'Confession'. For example, in Genesis chapter three Adam ad-

Studies in the First Epistle

mitted his sin but did not confess it. In fact he sought to blame his wife, and even God: 'The woman whom thou has given to me, she gave me to eat'. Confession and admission are not the same thing, neither are confession and regret. Confession is not even weeping bitter tears over sin, because sometimes we can weep tears over sin far more because of what it does to us, than what it does to God. That is a natural, not a spiritual thing to do. However when we do confess, John promises us that God is faithful and just to do two things: to forgive us and to cleanse us. Sin is not only an offence which needs forgiving, it is a pollution which needs cleansing. And John assures us that in our Lord Jesus Christ there is provision for both.

The third wrong attitude to sin. If the first is a form of libertinism, and the second is a form of escapism, the third is the error of perfectionism, which denies the presence of sin (v. 10). 'The seriousness,' says Calvin, 'of such exaggerated claims is that they blaspheme God by making him to be a liar, since we are contradicting God's statements about ourselves.' But such claims also exhibit, John says, that God's word has never really penetrated our hearts. This error of perfectionism in the sense of sinlessness derives from two things. Firstly from a stifling of conscience. The mark of the true man of God with a sensitive conscience that has not been stifled is that he grows more and more conscious of his sin and not less and less. But it's not only a stifling of conscience, it's an ignorance of God's word that produces it. Such people forget the very elementary thing that our Lord taught his disciples to pray, 'Forgive us our trespasses'. 'Daily bread,' says Jesus, 'and daily forgiveness' are the two basic needs of his disciples.

So it is that in chapter two (vv. 1, 2), John goes on to explain God's double provision for sin in his written word, and secondly, in the incarnate word. Two false deductions could be drawn from the previous section of John's letter. Either it could be concluded that since we shall never be rid of sin in this world, since the whole idea of sinlessness is a delusion, then there is no point in striving against it. Or it could be concluded that since remission of sins is so fully assured we can continue in sin (the error that Paul also deals with in his letter to the Romans (ch. 6)), whereas God's great purpose and his ultimate desire is to rid us of sin. And the great provision that God has made against sin, as stated here, is God's written word. The words, 'I am writing to you' refer to John's epistle primarily, but they are equally applicable to the whole of Scripture.

What is the basic key to a life of increasing victory over and freedom from sin? It is not to be found in some slick formula or some special blessing. It is to be found in a life steeped in and submitted to the word of the living God. And John then goes on in the latter part of verse one to state that if we fall into sin God has made provision for that too. Here is the beautiful balance between a wrong condoning of sin and a wrong despair about sin. John is saying that God wants to rid you of your sin (that is his ultimate aim) but if you do sin don't let it drive you from Jesus, instead let it drive you to him. Jesus is our propitiation and advocate. The metaphor he employs is a legal one. He sees God as our Father becoming in Jesus Christ our advocate to plead our cause and take up our case. Not like an earthly advocate who tries to say that we are not as bad as we are. He comes to his Father and says 'Father, look not upon them but upon me'. As he pleads the advocate becomes the accused, and the accused becomes the accursed, so that our advocate becomes our propitiation to procure our pardon and restore us to fellowship with God. This is how God has provided for his sinning children, so that when we fall we are to say in the words of the Prophet, 'Rejoice not against me O mine adversary, when I fall I shall rise again, when I sit in darkness the Lord shall be a light unto me for I have at God's right hand one who is even now pouring out the benefits of his death.'

2. The Evidence of Walking in the Light (2:3-29)

A new section of the epistle begins at verse three and goes on to the end of verse eleven. To put it in context it is to bring the assurance of eternal life to his readers, an assurance which is not only well grounded on God's word and on Christ's work, but also evidenced in the Christian's life. It is important to note that this evidential assurance, is, like all other assurance, grounded not on any achievement of our own. Evidential assurance is concerned not so much with what God has done in Christ, or what God has said in his word, as what God has brought in our own lives. So it is based still upon God and what he has done, but now upon what he has done *in* us. John gives us, for example, the test by which we may be sure that we know him (v. 3). In this first letter John is much concerned with these tests, so much so that we find the Apostle returning again and again to these basic tests, or evidences of eternal life. In this section *(vv. 3–11)* there are three of these tests, and in each case they are introduced with the phrase, 'He who says' (vv. 4, 5, 9). The point in each case is that mere profession, which is not supported by a consistent life, is sheer presumption. Or, to use John Stott's phrase, 'No religious experience is valid if it does not have moral consequences.' We can summarise the teaching of these first eleven verses in this way: 1. the evidence of *knowledge is obedience,* 2. the evidence of *union is likeness,* and 3. the evidence of *light is love.*

First, the evidence of knowing God is *obeying God.* Knowing God is one of the central thoughts in 1 John. It is something in the region of forty times in this epistle that you get one or other of the Greek words for *knowing.* If the Apostle's great concern is to confirm believers in possessing eternal life, one has to go on and say what is eternal life. Our Lord gives the answer, 'This is life eternal that they might know thee the only true God and Jesus Christ whom thou has sent' (John 17:3). Eternal life really consists in knowing God, and in the last analysis of course, this is what distinguishes the Christian from every other man. Paul in his letter to the Corinthians (1:21) says 'The world by wisdom did not know God', and to the Galatians 'You did not know God but now you have come to know him' (4:8, 9). The man who claims to know God like that must, says John, be able to produce a certain evidence that his whole life takes on a new shape and his great interest becomes not pleasing self, but pleasing God and obeying him. Obviously the test is not that the only man that knows God is the man who lives in perfect obedience to his every commandment. If it meant that, the only man who knows God is the man who perfectly keeps his commandments, then that would refer to one only, the Lord Jesus Christ. John Calvin has a wise and helpful comment on this: 'By keeping his commandments the Apostle does not mean that those who wholly satisfy the Lord God keep his commandments, for no such instance can be found in the world. He means rather those who desire to form their life in obedience to God.' It is what you really want deep down. Do I really want the whole will of God for the whole of my life? What God does in regeneration is not only to give us a new heart, he also puts his laws into our mind and writes them on our hearts. Thereafter there is a correspondence between the will of God and the deepest desire of the regenerate heart. John's point is that an habitual disregard of God's commandments, 'He who goes on disobeying his commandments', is utterly incompatible with knowing God. The evidence of knowing God is obeying God and verse five at the beginning is precisely what Jesus says in John's Gospel (14:15, 21, 23, 24).

Secondly, the evidence of union with Christ is *likeness to Christ*. There's a small grammatical point to notice at the end of verse five. In the A.V. the verse ends with a period. Whereas the R.S.V. ends with a colon. So that while the A.V. makes the last sentence look backwards, the R.S.V. makes it refer forwards to verse six. So the sense is, by this we may be sure that we are in him. By what? By this. 'He who says he abides in him ought to walk in the same way in which he walked.' Grammatically the sense could be either, but the context makes it more likely that the R.S.V. is right. The New English Bible translates it, 'Here is the test by which we can make sure that we are in him, whoever claims to be dwelling in him, binds himself to live as Christ himself lived.' What happens when you are converted is not just that you come to know God, but that you are united to him as the branches are to the vine (John 15). The point of that analogy is that the very same life found in the branches is found in the vine, so the fruit is the test.

The evidence of union with Christ is that, as John says, we walk (v. 6) in the same way in which he walked. In the perfect life of Jesus God magnified his law and made it honourable in the flesh of a man, the very place where it had been dishonoured and despised. So that every act, word and thought of Jesus was a perfect reflection of the character of God. And that perfect walk of our Lord has two important results for us. He thereby becomes a perfect Saviour, fitted to bear our sin, and he becomes a perfect example, so that we are to walk as he walked.

Thirdly the evidence of *light and love* (vv. 7 to 11). In verse nine we have the third description of what happens when someone becomes a Christian, 'Taken out of darkness into light'. John's main point in this passage is that there is a test of being brought to the light (John 13:34). Something of which one of the old Puritan commentators, John Cotton, says: 'Here the Apostle poses for us a conundrum, he speaketh of a commandment which is new yet old, and of a commandment which is true in him and true in you.' What is the solution to the conundrum? It is that here John is speaking of the commandment Jesus gave which is old, in that they have heard it from the beginning of the gospel era, yet it was new as the distinctive hallmark of Christian discipleship, 'By this shall all men know that you are my disciples if you love one another.' This is the distinctive commandment for the new age. But you will notice this commandment is said to be true in him and true in you. John's point is that the love by which our lives are tested is not a human phenomenon, like being philanthropic. It is loving others as Jesus loved us. This is the new commandment for the new age which Jesus said had already dawned (v. 8). Here then is the great test. Light and love belong together, and here he sets it down as the basic evidence of Christian grace. This warm spirit of self-giving towards others which is Christian love. The cold, hard, distant heart, the sense of forbidding detachment from other people, is a contrary sign of Christian grace. It is a contradiction of the evidence for which God the Holy Spirit is looking in our lives. Love and hatred says the Apostle are as incompatible as light and darkness and he states this principle, first negatively and then positively. 'He who says he is in the light and hates his brother is in the darkness still' (v. 9). 'He who loves his brother abides in the light and in him there is no cause of stumbling' (v. 10). That last phrase at the end of verse ten and then into verse eleven is the point at which John extends this teaching to the influence the light, or darkness, exerts upon us. Thus, at the end of verse ten, 'The man who loves and who is therefore in the light has nothing in him which will make him stumble, he sees clearly and walks wisely and uprightly, he who loves his brother abides in the light.' And it's more likely to be in 'him' than in 'it', which is how the R.S.V. translates it. But in verse eleven, the man whose heart is full of hatred finds that his whole view of things and people is so distorted that he is fumbling and stumbling in the darkness. He who hates his brother does not know where he is going because the darkness has blinded his eyes. The evidence of the loveless heart is that it is almost incapable of seeing the good in other people. Dr. David Smith says, 'The penalty of living in the darkness is not merely that one does not see, but that one goes blind.' 'Such a man,' wrote Robert Law, 'does not perceive the true character of his own actions.' The selfish man is ignorant of any notion that he is selfish. The quarrelsome person thinks

Studies in the First Epistle

that everyone is unreasonable except himself, the revengeful that he is animated only by a proper self-respect, even if he does observe that his relation to his brother is somewhat out of joint he goes on imputing to him all the wrong and the mischief. The roots of which are really in himself because the darkness had blinded his eyes. The penalty of walking in the darkness is the extinction of vision. And the work of God is full of this truth: 'He who will not see at last cannot.'

These next three verses (12, 13, 14) are clearly a word of encouragement, a very important balance to the solemnity of these challenging tests. A balance we need to preserve. (If we are always encouraging people we will tend to leave them in a situation of soporific rest. If we are always challenging and disturbing people we will bring them into a situation of despair, but the word of God marries together the two.) John is writing in these terms of seeking evidences for our knowing Christ, for our being united with Christ, for our walking in the light. John is seeking these evidences, which I have been referring to not to depress them or discourage them, nor because he has a gloomy view of their spiritual state. So in these verses, which have a clear structure he tells them so. John makes six statements. Three of them are introduced with the words 'I am writing' (R.S.V.). The next three are introduced with the phrase 'I write to you' (R.S.V.). What John is doing is referring to what he has been writing to them and is still writing to them in the Epistle. What he writes is addressed to what looks like three categories of people: children, young men and fathers. Two questions arise about these categories and I will comment on each. How many are they? And, who are they? Well let me answer both these questions quickly. I have always regarded these as three categories of people, as descriptions not of physical age but of spiritual growth. I have been increasingly persuaded recently that John's opening mode of address, 'Little children', is his general address to all his readers, not to one particular category. Then he goes on to divide them into two categories, fathers and young men. The reason I incline to that view is because the phrase 'Little children', occurs on seven other occasions throughout this epistle and they refer to all John's readers in general.

With the first general term of endearment to his little children, he writes a word of encouragement about their spiritual state. 'I am writing to you little children because your sins are forgiven you for his sake' and, 'I write to you children because you know the Father.' These are two great foundation stones on which you all rest, your sins have been forgiven you and you have been brought to know God. This is what distinguishes the believer from the man of the world, of whom he is about to write (v. 15). There are times when you and I also need to stand back and allow God to say that to us. 'You are my child, and I have brought you to myself into fellowship with me and all your sins are gone.' That is where we begin with God.

After that general statement, he particularises. First of all, the fathers. He says the same thing to them on both occasions. 'I am writing to you fathers because you know him who is from the beginning.' That is very significant. These are doubtless believers of some spiritual stature and spiritual growth, and the mark of their growth is that they have grown in the knowledge of God. The point John is making is: that is the only kind of Christian growth that is worth talking about. It is the grand obsession of the life of Apostle Paul; 'that I

Studies in the First Epistle

may know him.' 'I write to you young men because you have overcome the evil one' (v. 13); 'because you are strong and the word of God abides in you and you have overcome the evil one' (v. 14). In other words, there are those growing into maturity who are engaged in all the battles and conflicts of Christian living, and what rejoices John's heart is that he sees them victorious over the evil one and he encourages them by reminding them of their victories and particularly of the source of them. This is a great ministry to people who are in the midst of a sense of failure, or facing some conflict. Encouragement is not a cheap form of flattery, because neither the victory nor the strength by which they attained it, is their own. Look at the juxtaposition in verse fourteen, 'You are strong' and 'the word of God abides in you.' That is what makes for victorious Christian living, when the word of God abides in us. That is the permanent testimony of our Lord's experience with the evil one in the wilderness.

Here are some brief lessons from these verses. There is such a thing, first of all, as progress in Christian experience, growth in grace. So we are to deal with people as John clearly does according to the stage they are at. 'I was gentle among you as a nurse with her children,' writes Paul. Do you know what it is to have that gentle long-suffering patience that fractious children need? There are many unsteady young believers who greatly need an unselfish 'nurse-maid'. Second, this progress of growth is gradual, as in human growth, so our great concern in any fellowship should be to help and encourage one another to grow. And it's not without significance that growth takes place best in a family. The third lesson, the nature of this growth is growing in the knowledge of God, 'You know the father'. So the chief business of the Christian's life is knowing God. The devil's chief business will be to keep us from knowing God, and that is why the devil keeps you from reading your Bible. Fourthly, the chief means of this growth, and of becoming strong in the Lord, is the word of God abiding in you.

Now we go on to these next three verses (15 to 17). John has been gaining a vantage point from which to urge them on still further, particularly in relation to their attitude to the world, so we should not interpret his encouragement as meaning that he is contented with them where they are. He says to them 'Now having taken our encouragement from God, let's go on to face another situation that we need to deal with in our lives.' That is his warning in verse fifteen 'Do not love the world or the things in the world.' There are two meanings for the word 'world' in Scripture. The one in John 3:16 is world in the sense of the whole human race. But the other in 1 John 2:15 is the godless world as the New English Bible translates it. What Professor C. H. Dodd calls 'The life of human society as it is organised under the power of evil.' This is the world to which John is referring: human society orientated against God. There is no ambiguity in John's teaching about the relationship of the Christian to the world in this sense. You will either love the Father he says or you will love the world. He is speaking about something which is a spirit, a deep seated sinister spirit that invades every area of our lives. It's not just the one or two things that some people use to identify a worldly Christian. But what John is speaking about is a worldly spirit that can invade every area of our lives. Robert Law offers this comment: 'God lays down one programme of life for his children, the world proposes another and totally in-

Studies in the First Epistle

compatible programme for its servants. So love for the one excludes love for the other.' John particularises this programme as 'Lust of the flesh, lust of the eyes, and the pride of life' (v. 16).

A brief look at each of these. *'The lust of the flesh,'* is the whole world of appetite and the gratifying of sinful desires. It is the debasing of bodily appetites, not the appetites themselves. These bodily appetites that God has given us are altogether wholesome whether they be for food, sex or sleep. They are all good and as God gives them he can sanctify them. The appetite for food can be sanctified so that it becomes a cause for gratitude to God, that's why we say grace before we eat. It can become a means of grace to us. Similarly the satisfying of the sexual appetite, within the bounds of marriage, can become sanctified by God as an expression of that precious gift of human love. It is something that is glorifying to God when it is rightly used, that is what makes the prostitution of it such a tragedy. Similarly, the desire for sleep can be something that can be glorifying to God and something God gives us. But the devil can debase these appetites, for food into gluttony, for sex into lust, and for sleep into sloth. The lust of the flesh is to allow these appetites to consume you for selfish ends. *'The lust of the eyes'* is the lust after the superficial. C. H. Dodd describes this as the 'Tendency to be captivated by the outward show of things without enquiring into their true value.' *'The pride of life,'* is the empty glory of this world. It is pretentious and ostentatious and desires to impress with the superficial, whether it is wealth, rank, dress, house or academic achievement. The people who indulge in this kind of vanity are giving away what really matters to them in life. 'If a man loves the world,' said Jesus, 'the love of the Father is not in him.' Someone has suggested that these three together may be summed up as either an unholy desire for what one does not have, or an unholy pride in what one does have. The second main reason for not loving the world is that the world is passing away, it is in the process of decay (v. 17). That is a universal Biblical comment on the world and its glory. It is passing not permanent. Remember the words of our Lord, 'Lay not up for yourselves treasure on earth where moth and rust corrupt and thieves break through a steal.' Because the things of this world are passing they are transient.

In the last sections (vv. 18 to 27) John returns to the tests or evidences of possessing eternal life, and introduces a new test. Much of what we so far have been studying has been concerned with the right behaviour of the Christian. But now he turns to the test of right belief. Christians not only have a relation to God, to one another and to the world, they have a relation to the truth. And here John is emphasising the test of our relation to the truth (v. 22). This section may be divided into four parts. The heretics of whom John speaks are identified and described (vv. 18, 19). Christians are identified and described by contrast (vv. 20, 21). The nature of their error is exposed (vv. 22, 23). And, the safeguards against error are described (vv. 24–27). John introduces the first part with the words 'It is the last hour'. Here he is pointing to the fact that with the coming of Christ the last stage of world history has begun. He is not suggesting that we are about to come to the moment of our Lord's return at this point, because it was not the last hour. (Our Lord had told his disciples in Mark chapter thirteen that no one knows the time of the last hour.) But what he is saying is that before the

Studies in the First Epistle

final consumation the Lord had led his disciples to expect that there would be evidences of his foes conspiring against him. 'False Christs and false prophets will arise and show signs and wonders to lead us stray, if possible the elect' (Mark 13:22). In that sense it was the last hour, and still is the last hour. Professor Blaiklock in his studies in 1 John says, 'Nothing is so damaging in the study of New Testament prophecy as to imagine that the eternal God who stands outside and above time is bound by the clocks and calendars of men.' John describes these heretics as 'many anti-Christs' (v. 18), and he identifies them as 'nominal members of the church' (v. 19). So these are not demons, they are men. These men are called *anti-christs* because they take their character from the anti-christ of whom he speaks in verses eighteen and twenty-two. Hidden here in the statement 'They were not of us, because if they had been of us they would have continued with us,' is the test of Christian perseverance. The Greek word for 'continue' is the regular word for Christian continuance and is a test of genuineness. For example, 'If you continue in my word, then are you my disciples indeed.' So there is their identification and description. The second part states that Christians are identified and described by contrast. It is characteristic of John to place two contrasting parties side by side (vv. 18, 19 and 20, 21). The Christ and his *anti-christs*. The Anointed, which is what Christ means, and his anointed ones. The word 'anointing' is the Greek word *Chrisma*, and it is closely associated to the word 'Christ'. Christ was anointed at his baptism by the Holy Spirit, and John is probably emphasising here that every Christian, not the select few as these heretics were saying, has the anointing of the Holy Spirit. It is Christ himself who anoints us. Plummer says in his commentary, 'All Christians are in a secondary sense, what Christ is in a primary sense, the Lord's anointed.' Verse twenty-seven elaborates the fact that this anointing or gift of the Holy Spirit is the pre-requisite of knowing the truth. 'They know the truth from error because they possess the Holy Spirit.' Thirdly, the nature of their error is exposed in verses twenty-two and twenty-three. Who is this liar? It is he who denies that Jesus is the Christ. That does not mean that they denied Jesus of Nazareth was the Mesiah, because they distinguished between Jesus and the Christ. The suggestion these heretics were making was that on the man Jesus the divine anointing came at his baptism, but left him before his crucifixion. To John the lie *par-excellence* is that which refuses to see the Godhead shine in the human life and saving death of Jesus. This obviously refers to heretical sects today. The key question always is what they say about the personal work of Christ. It also has a reference to comparative religion, when people will say, 'Do not all religions lead to God?' Finally, consider the twofold protection against their error (vv. 24, 25). When John says, 'If what you heard from the beginning abides in you then you will abide in the Son and the Father,' he is referring to the word of the gospel which they heard from the beginning. That is, apostolic truth which for us today is inscripturated in holy writ. Then in verses twenty-six and twenty-seven he refers to the anointing which we receive from God, clearly a reference to the Holy Spirit. So what is the twofold protection against error? It is the Holy Scripture and the Holy Spirit. Both are necessary if we are going to be preserved for God. The word needs the Spirit and the Spirit needs the word, for the word of

God is the sword of the Spirit. Sometimes we emphasise the Spirit instead of the word. Some of us would emphasise the word and neglect the Spirit. But we may do neither. What God has joined together let not his people put asunder.

3. The Privileges and Obligations of being children of God (3:1 – 4:6)

The last verse of chapter two seems to be connected more with what follows than with what precedes it and the link is the phrase at the end of the verse, 'Born of him.' We are still dealing with John's great concern to see the evidence of eternal life in a professing believer and he now returns to the tests previously referred to, but like the spiral staircase which is the symbol for John's form of teaching he returns to it at a higher level. Previously, the test was put in the form, 'If you truly have fellowship with God who is light, you will walk in the light'. Now it is put in the form, 'If you are truly born of God who is righteous, you will practice righteousness'. There is also a link with the twenty-eighth verse of chapter two. We are urged to abide in him so that when he appears we may have confidence and not shrink from him in shame at his coming. He will be looking for the reflection of the Father's nature in the children's character because we are born of God. John's language about the new birth is the kind someone would use in an excited way when they had dis-

Studies in the First Epistle

covered something when it was really worth calling everybody's attention to. The sort of thing that happens sometimes when you may be climbing a high hill and suddenly you turn and look round and everybody's facing upwards towards the top of the hill, and you say to them, 'Just turn and look at this'. The Apostle, suddenly aware of this vista of the love of God says, 'Behold, look, turn your eyes upon this'. John Cotton the New England Puritan commentator says, 'The Apostle desireth to correct our squint'. 'Behold' we read in the A.V., 'what manner of love the Father hath bestowed upon us.' Which literally means, 'From what country is this love?' The idea behind it is that this is something for which we have no parallel in our world. One of the devil's quieter and more subtle tactics is to dull this sense of wonder in the minds of God's children. I find this very significant because we often think that the time when all this comes home to us with the greatest sense of wonder is when it's all new and fresh to us, like William Cowper, who cries in his hymn, 'Where is the blessedness I knew when first I saw the Lord?' But the Apostle John we see writing here is a very old man. He has probably been a believer for something like sixty years and yet he has never lost the sense of sheer wonder at the love of God. I think that sense of wonder is a great index of the heart.

If we are going to see the wonder of this, we need to think it through together. What is this love of God by which we are both named and made sons of God? Where do we see it, where does the wonder of it really lie? I suggest that we see the core of the wonder of God's love in three specific acts of God's grace whereby he makes us his sons and they all can be inferred from this epistle. We become sons of God first of all, by *substitution,* or *propitiation.* The Scripture tells us that by nature we are the children of wrath, and where God's amazing love is seen is in how he takes those who are children of wrath and constitutes them sons of God. And in the astonishing mystery of God's substitutionary atoning work he makes the Son of his love the object of his wrath, so that the children of wrath might become the sons of his love. The second word which illuminates what kind of love God bestowed on us to make us his children is *adoption.* That is to say that we are not sons of God by nature, but sons by grace. Did you ever see one of these announcements in the paper when someone has adopted a child and they say 'chosen son of so-and so'. I think it's a beautiful way to describe an adoption. We are called children of God because we are chosen sons and daughters of his, and adopted into all the privileges and blessings and status of his family. Yet there is more to it even than that. Propitiation and adoption are not all. We become sons of God also by *regeneration,* that is by the new birth. The Apostle says, 'See what love the Father has given us that we shall be called the children of God.' But there is more than that, and in the R.S.V. he goes on 'And so we are'. What does he mean by that? He means that we are not only called by that name, but we have been born into that family. The connection between adoption and regeneration is this, that whereas by adoption we receive all the privileges and status of being his children, by regeneration we receive the nature of his children. Now says John, at the end of verse one, 'Don't be surprised that the world is quite blind to what it means to be a child of God. The reason why the world does not know us is that it did not know him. It was blind to God's only begotten Son.'

Studies in the First Epistle

John having spoken of the present dignity of the children of God, goes on to speak about our future destiny. The two are always bound together in the New Testament (v. 2 and Romans 8: the same juxtaposition, 'If children, then heirs, heirs of God and joint heirs with Christ.') But if our present privileges are beyond the wit of the world, our future prospects defy even the understanding of the redeemed. 'It does not yet appear what we shall be' says the Apostle. God has not unfolded it to us yet and the reason he has not, Martin Luther says, is that we could not on our earthly spirits bear the wonder of it. But what we do know is that when he appears we shall be like him. Perhaps that is why our Lord prayed 'That they may behold my glory' (John 17). For when we do we shall be changed into his likeness. Such a blessed hope John goes on to tell us (v. 3) has present practical implications. Everyone who thus hopes in him purifies himself as he is pure. While it remains true that only the blood of Christ can purify us, what John is emphasising is that we are not inactive in our sanctification. It is the blood of Christ that goes on cleansing us we found in chapter one. 'It is God who is at work in you,' says the Apostle Paul (Phil. 2:13). What is the conclusion we can draw from that? Do we just sit back and do nothing? That may be a logical conclusion but it's not a Biblical one, and it's better to be Biblical and illogical than to be logical and unbiblical. Paul replies that God is at work in you, so work out your own salvation. And John writes 'Purify yourselves as he is pure.'

As we turn to verses four to ten let me point out the link to you. In the previous verses John has seen the second appearing of Christ as a great motive to holiness (v. 3). But here (vv. 4 to 10) the motive to holiness is drawn not from Christ's second appearing, but from his first appearing (vv. 5, 8). It is highly significant that both the appearings of Christ have our righteous behaviour in view. There is a symmetry about these verses. They contain two statements about sin, about Christ's appearing, and about the believer.

First of all, the two statements about sin (vv. 4, 8).
1. It is lawlessness, a violation of God's law, and its origin is of the devil. It appears that these heretics, to whom I referred in our first study, totally disregarded the category of law in their thinking. Plummer, in the Cambridge Bible for Schools, says, 'They thought their superior enlightenment placed them above the moral law. They were neither the better for keeping it, nor the worse for breaking it.' But John says sin and lawlessness are interchangeable terms, and he identifies sin as rebellion against God's law. Dr. John Robinson, the former Bishop of Woolwich, is only speaking a half truth when he describes sin as 'a failure to love'. Now that's a very common theological way of describing sin today. But it is highly significant that John, the 'Apostle of Love', describes sin not so much as lovelessness as lawlessness. If its nature is lawlessness the other thing he says about sin is that its origin is of the devil (v. 8). More accurately it is the origin of the sinner that's here described, and John's contrast is between the family of God and the family of the devil. Members of both families are known by their moral likeness to their head.

2. The two statements about Christ's appearing (5 & 8b). The sinless one appeared to take away sin (later in this chapter we learn that he did so by laying down his life for us), and to destroy the works of the devil. Christ's appearing was not just to deal with our sins

Studies in the First Epistle

which needed forgiving, but with the whole kingdom of evil which he came to break up and to destroy. Together, you get the whole work of redemption.

3. The two statements about the believer (vv. 6, 7, 9, 10). First, in verse six, if the nature of Jesus is sinless, his purpose is to take away sin, then the believer will recognise how utterly incompatible sin is with abiding in Christ. Secondly, in verses nine and ten, he draws the conclusion that if you are a child of God, rather than a child of the devil, then the whole disposition of your life will reflect God's nature rather than the devil's. Now these verses have caused difficulty amongst interpreters. The difficulty arises with the phrase in verse nine: 'He cannot sin', and 'no one born of God commits sin'. I want to take time here to examine that verse. The difficulty has been solved by people in various ways. (i) It has been interpreted to say that John is actually telling us that it is not only inconsistent for a born again Christian to sin, but impossible. I would suggest, however, that it is obvious that John would not be contradicting what he previously said in the first chapter, 'If we say we have not sinned, we deceive ourselves.' And in the second chapter, 'If any man sin (that is, he at least allows the possibility) we have an advocate with the Father.' So that is a very inconsistent interpretation. (ii) Another which is more common is that John is distinguishing between the old and the new nature of the believer. (Whereas the old nature may continue to sin the new nature cannot sin.) The difficulty here is that the language will not bear that interpretation, because the subject of the verbs, 'Commit sin' and 'Cannot sin', is not one of the believer's nature, but the believer as a person born of God. (iii) This last interpretation has two points to be noted. The first is that you have

to recognise which error the Apostle is combating in order to understand what he is saying. On the one hand, some of these heretics denied the presence of sin in them, and suffering from moral blindness they needed to be undeceived so he presses on them the universality of sin. But on the other hand, others were careless about sin, they were morally indifferent. To the first group John emphasises one thing, to the second he emphasises the incompatibility of sin in the life of the Christian. But the other thing, which seems to me even more important, is that the tense John uses in verse nine, 'No one born of God commits sin,' is a tense which refers not to isolated acts but to persistence in sin. Professor Blaiklock comments, 'The present tense in the Greek verb implies habit, continuity, unbroken sequence.' And he renders John's expressions in the ninth verse in the same way as the New International Version 'He does not practice sin, he cannot continue sinning.'

Taking the teaching of the epistle as a whole John's general position is that a Christian may fall into sin but he will not walk in it. And at the end of verse ten, we have a link with the next section of the chapter when John gathers together what he has been saying about the privileges and obligations of being children of God, and then at the end of the verse he introduces, almost imperceptibly, the theme of love, not God's love to us but our love to others (vv. 11 to 18). Plummer points out the ease of the transition by saying that 'Whereas obedience is righteousness in relation to God, love is righteousness in relation to others.' After introducing the theme as being of the essence of the original teaching of Jesus (this is the message that you have heard from the beginning that we should love one another), John presents two strikingly contrasting illustrations to set out the two possible relationships between men. One illustration comes from Cain (v. 12) and the other from Christ (v. 16). The whole challenge of these verses is this: that we all, in our attitude to others are either like Cain or like Christ. John sees Cain and Christ, as Robert Law puts it, as prototypes of hate and love, of the world and the Church, of the children of God and the children of the devil. This is a significant and searching test, because it is so often in our relationships with other people that we are tested. Paul includes sanctification in so many of his epistles in terms of relationships – children to their parents, husbands to their wives, masters to their servants. It is in that realm that the real issues are faced and fought out. Look, for example, at John's diagnosis of the cause of Cain's act (v. 12). Why did he murder his brother? John Cotton says, 'The Apostle catechiseth himself.' Why did he murder him? John asks himself. And the answer is: because his own deeds were evil and his brother's righteous. Have you got that? He murdered him because his own deeds were evil and his brother's righteous. Robert Law has this penetrating comment, 'The goodness he refused to emulate became unendurable, it goaded his self-love to madness.' So often our love is really tested at this point and how it reacts to the blessing and the preferment and the recognition of another. I used to think when I read that phrase in Romans about 'weeping with those who weep' and 'rejoicing with those who rejoice' that the real test of a man's love for another was if he was genuinely able to weep with those who weep. But I now think that the real test is if he is genuinely able to rejoice with those who rejoice when perhaps he does not have the same cause for it. Cain, in particular, and the world in general, reveal their spiritual deadness by their attitude to others, says John (v. 15): 'Anyone who hates his brother is a murderer and you know that no murderer has eternal life abiding in him.' John sees little distinction, just as Jesus, between hatred and murder because hatred, as our Lord told us in the Sermon on the Mount, reveals the same moral attitude as murder. Comments Calvin, 'We hate people because we wish to dispose of them out of the world.'

By contrast, we know love when we look at the example of Christ (v. 16). You will notice that there is a further contrast between Cain and Christ implied in this verse, 'By this we know love that he laid down his life for us'. And he laid down his life for us when we were still sinners. So Christ's example of love, is love in the face of evil and in response to it (contrasted by Cain's self-love driving him to murder in the face of righteousness). And this is the example we are called to emulate. We often think of this kind of love as an unattainable ideal because our circumstances are never ideal. But there is no ideal set of circumstances in which to exercise Christian love. Just as, contrary to what we often think, there is no ideal set of circumstances in which to live the Christian life. And so John says, 'By this we know love that he laid down his life for us and we ought to lay down our lives for our brethren.' But the laying down of our lives is an obligation that is laid on very few. So John goes on to spell out this homelier test of Christian love, 'If anyone has the world's goods and sees his brother in need, yet closes his heart against him, how does God's love abide in him?' In some circumstances it may be easier to die for others than to live for others. Dr. David Smith says, 'It's easy in some

Studies in the First Epistle

cases to lay down one's life, martyrdom can be heroic and exhilarating.' Though I don't think I would find it so. 'But,' he says, 'the difficulty lies in doing the little things, facing day by day the petty sacrifices and self-denials which no one notices and no one applauds.' John's concluding exhortation in verse eighteen does not mean that love does not sometimes express itself in word or speech. His point is that this will not be the only kind of expression. Mere words are no evidence of either faith or love (James 2:15, 16).

The next section is verses nineteen to twenty-four, which could be entitled, in Bishop Westcott's phrase, 'The fruit of love is confidence'. Here again you have an illustration of what we have already found in this epistle, the beautiful balance of God's truth. What the Apostle has just been saying about love is chastening and challenging, so he turns once more to the ministry of encouragement, 'Lest someone should despair.' You will notice that the passage begins and ends with the phrase, 'By this we shall know' (vv. 19, 24). You can just imagine, as doubtless John was doing, someone listening to these words he has just written and saying to themselves, 'I don't love as I ought to. Lord can I really be your child at all?' It's interesting that the New English Bible quite properly renders 'heart' as 'conscience' in verse nineteen. Our conscience is not an infallible guide. God is a greater and better judge and John's point is that we are to appeal from our conscience to God as a higher court because God sees down into the hidden depths of our hearts. There are times when we need to come to God with the language of the man who once wrote, 'Lord I am not what I ought to be, I am certainly not what I want to be, neither am I what one day by thy grace I shall be, but blessed be the Lord, I am not what I used to be.' That is one of the ways we are to reassure our hearts before God. We come to him and say, 'Lord thou knowest all things, look into my heart. You know that I long to be like Jesus and to love men as Jesus loved them.' And God says 'My child, I see it, I know, I know.' It is important to add that there is such a thing as a morbid conscience, which is the nagging, niggling voice of the devil as the accuser of the brethren who is determined to give you no peace. Of course, conscience is God's monitor in the soul, but the Spirit of God does not speak to his children with a harsh, strident, unrelenting, nagging tone. That is the voice of the accuser. Jesus said, 'My sheep know my voice', and you and I have to learn the distinction. The important thing is that this reassuring of our hearts is done before God. The worldling or the hypocrite may drug his conscience, but he can never do so before God. In verses twenty-one and twenty-two, one of the evil results of the condemning conscience is that it keeps us from coming before God in prayer. 'We have confidence,' writes John. Boldness is another way that the word is translated. It literally means, 'Freedom of speech at the throne of Grace.' Quite obviously, the Apostle is not saying in verse twenty-two that our prayers are answered as a reward for keeping God's commandments. But it is true that obedience is a pre-requisite of prayer, and that brings a solution to the whole question that arises from that verse when we say, do we really receive from him whatever we ask. John links it with obedience. The two are linked together supremely (boldness before the throne, and obedience to the Father) in the life of Jesus (John 8:29 aid 11:41). The connection between our assurance of being heard and receiving what we ask on the one hand, and our obedience to his will on the other. Maybe that when our lives are in harmony with our Father's will, our praying will be too. This twofold commandment, we keep his commandents and do what pleases him, is spelled out in verse twenty-three. It is faith in Christ and love to the brethren.

At the end of this chapter John gathers all this teaching up in terms of abiding in Christ (v. 24). It is, of course, full of significance that in John 15, which is obviously much in John's mind in this epistle, you get the same marks of evidences of abiding in him. Abiding in Christ is not some mystical experience which we may loosely claim. We are only constantly abiding when we are consistently obeying and selflessly loving.

The final clause in chapter three leads us into the first six verses of chapter four. The evidence of God abiding in us is the presence and ministry of the Holy Spirit. 'By this we know he abides in us by the Spirit which he has given us.' So we are to reassure our hearts before God by looking for the evidence of the Holy Spirit's working in our lives, enabling us to obey God's Commandments, to believe in the name of his Son and to love one another. But John sounds out a warning (4:1) that there are other spirits besides the Holy Spirit, '. . . do not believe every spirit but test the spirits . . .' What John is saying is that not every supernatural manifestation is to be regarded as the spirit which he has given us. G. G. Finley in his exposition of 1 John warns us that 'to identify the supernatural and the divine is a perilous mistake', and we greatly need to heed that warning in our own generation. So John urges that every spirit should be subjected to testing to see whether it is truly of God. Now the necessity of doing so seems to derive from the fact that it is highly possible even for Christian people to be deceived by what John calls 'the spirit of anti-Christ' (v. 3). The Greek word used here for testing, *dokimadzine*, is the word used for testing a coin to see if it was a fake. The reason people test a banknote is not because it is an obvious forgery. They test it because it is very convincing and might even deceive the banker. So John says, we test the spirits because they are liable to deceive even the elect. Indeed one gets the impression in these six verses of a deep-seated war between two sides, the one seeking to deceive and the other seeking to lead into the truth. First, 'By this you know the Spirit of God (vv. 2, 3). Then in verse three, 'The spirit of anti-Christ.' In verse four, 'He who is in you and he who is in the world.' Then in verse six, 'The Spirit of truth and the spirit of error.'

It is not surprising that verse four has a military flavour about it, 'Have overcome them.' The evil one is out to deceive and destroy and he sends out his emissaries for this reason. 'Many false prophets have gone out into the world' *(v. 1)*. It's very striking to think of our Lord commanding his disciples, 'Go ye into all the world and preach the Gospel', and almost as a diabolical echo the devil saying to his false prophets, 'Go ye out into all the world and deceive'. There is no question about these false prophets being inspired, but the question is, who inspired them?

Here are John's tests. In verses two and three the test is their confession of Christ. The word for 'confess' is the same word as used for confessing sin, therefore, it is not simply acknowledging Christ anymore than confessing sin is simply admitting it. This is to say the same things about Jesus as God says about him. It is the idea of honouring him, yielding to him, obeying him, and fashioning our lives according to his will. All this is

Studies in the First Epistle

involved in confessing him. The second test (vv. 5, 6) is of their heroes. These prophets are to be tested not only by what they say but by who listens to them (v. 6). Compare this with, whoever knows God listens to us. There appears to be a correspondence, in other words, between the message and the heroes. The popularity of a movement is not therefore by itself evidence of its spirituality. And the contrast between these two teachers, they who are of the world and we who are of God, is the last test. The 'they' of verse five are clearly false prophets, but 'we' in verse six almost certainly refers not to Christians in general but to the Apostles in particular. And that would be of great significance because for us the Apostolic teaching today is enshrined in Holy Scripture so that the touchstone of truth and error for us is the written word of God.

A final comment on verse four. In the midst of all this conflict, this pressure that they are under from truth and error John says, 'Little children, you are of God and you have overcome them. For he who is in you is greater than he who is in the world.' In all this bewilderment he is reminding them again of the thing we constantly need to remind ourselves, 'Greater is he that is in you than he that is in the world.' This is the ground on which we are able to be more than conquerors. It is the glorious truth that over against the very worst that the devil can throw at God's people there stands this incontrovertible fact that we are indwelt by One who is greater than anything else that can stand against us. We need that kind of vision which Elisha prayed for his servant when he told him, 'More are they that be for us than they that be for them.' And he said 'Lord, open the young man's eyes.'

4. The Implications of Abiding in Love Conclusion: The Full Assurance of Faith (4:7 – 5:21)

In this final section John returns to the theme of loving one another but at a higher level of the spiral staircase. This time the command to love is related to the alternate thing which is the nature and character of God himself, and what he has done for us in his Son (vv. 7, 8, 16). Indeed the thrice repeated exhortation 'Love one another' is based upon three grounds to which John appeals.

In the first place, we are to love one another because this is what God is like in his nature (v. 7). Secondly, we are to love one another because this is how God has revealed himself in his Son (v. 9). And thirdly, we are to love one another because this is how God reveals himself through his people (v. 12). And here I would comment: You will notice in verse seven 'Love is from God' (the literal translation); that is, he is the source of it. And verse eight 'God is love'; that is, this is his very essence. But we need to know what we are saying when we say that God is love. The New Testament writers when they wanted to speak of God's love bypassed the usual Greek words like *eros* from which we get our word erotic and used the word *agape*. Dr. Leon Morris says, 'They used a new term because they had a new idea to convey.' So when John is speaking about God's love he is speaking about something which is exclusive to God and foreign to natural man.

Human love has at least two main characteristics. First it is roused by something in its object. So we speak not only about our loving, but about things or people being lovable. Secondly, it includes the desire to get as well as to give. Divine love, by contrast, is roused by nothing outside of itself, and therefore loves the unlovely and the unlovable. It is all give. And when that kind of love begins to be seen in a human life it is evidence of the new birth, says John, and of fellowship with God. Contrarywise when there is no evidence of it, the claim to know God is an empty claim. In John Stott's words, 'For the loveless Christian to claim to know God and to have been born of God is like claiming to be intimate with a foreigner whose language we cannot speak, or to have been born of parents whom we do not in any way remember.' Somebody asked me this question the other day: If we have God's nature when we are born again, will it not be entirely natural for us to love, as it is for someone who has his parents' nature? If that is so, why does John plead with us to love? In other words, if we have God's nature and God is love, is it not a natural thing for us to love? And why is the Apostle having to plead with us to love? The answer is that although in a sense it is natural (our new nature is given to us) it is not automatic. This is the distinction. We have to exercise ourselves to love.

Secondly, we are to love one another because this is how God has revealed himself in his Son. What John means is that if we are to understand Christian love, we must not begin from the human side. We will never really understand the greatness of God's love, until we have seen that it was love to those who were the objects of God's wrath, which is what the word *propitiation* implies. That is what makes sin serious. What makes sin serious for men is not what sin does to me, although in all conscience that is desperately serious. Neither is it what sin does to other people, although it creates havoc in other people. But the thing that makes sin really serious is what it does to God. It draws down from God upon men his holy and abiding wrath. Hence Paul begins his exposition of the gospel in Romans by saying, 'The wrath of God is revealed from heaven against all ungodliness and wickedness of men.' What Christ bore was the just judgement of a holy God upon sin, and the significance of this word *propitiation* is that he bore the wrath of God for us. That is why he cries out in that moment of desolation, 'My God, my God, why hast thou forsaken me?' It was the love of God that devised such a salvation for sinners, and nowhere else in the universe do you see these two things brought together so starkly. God is light and God is love, and it is in Christ's propitiatory sacrifice that we see God as light and love acting for me. There is a weak and romantic idea of the love of God which says, God's love is such that he just forgives us our sins without requiring this ugly idea of his Son bearing his wrath. James Denny once wrote, 'God is love, say the Apostles, for he provides a propitiation.' And that is what John is saying. In verse eleven he draws the conclusion, that if God so loved us, if this is the love of God that we have tasted, we also ought to love one another. God's love in Christ, in other words, is the main spring of Christian love. Now we can see why it is that this love is so specific to people who have been brought to the cross of Jesus. However, some people find difficulty with the word 'ought' in this verse, with the idea of love being commanded, which is cousin to the previous question. But this love is not just an emotion, a sort of tingling sensation which periodically creeps up the believing spine. The kind of love that John is speaking about is a wilful commitment of ourselves to others for Christ's sake. Or, to use John Stott's memorable phrase, 'Christian love is not the victim of our emotions, but the servant of our will.'

Thirdly, we are to love one another not only because this is what God is like in his nature, and how God has revealed himself in his Son, but we are to love one another because this is how God reveals himself through his people. The phrase, 'No man has ever seen God' (v. 12) John previously used in his gospel where he says this in order to highlight the fact that the invisible God is made visible in his Son (John 1:18). But here we are being told that the invisible God who has revealed himself historically in Christ, reveals himself contemporarily in people when they love one another. That is a wonderful and glorious statement. John boldly says that this is where the love of God is brought to its maturity. We need to take this with great seriousness because the way that man who has not seen God, and who lives without the Bible today, is going to see God made visible in the loving, outgoing lives of his own redeemed people, particularly in their relation to one another.

John again takes up the two phrases at the end of the previous paragraph 'God abides in us' and 'His love is perfected in us' and expounds them in this next section

(vv. 13–21). It is a continuation of the teaching in many ways. First (vv. 13–16) the mutual indwelling of the believer in God, and God in the believer, is mentioned three times. And on each of these occasions God provides us with the evidence of this mutual abiding. It is the gift of the Holy Spirit (v. 13), it is the confession of Jesus as the Son of God (v. 15), and it is abiding in love, which is the test of abiding in God (v. 16). Dean Alfred points out that in Scripture the possession of the Holy Spirit is always tested by his fruit. And since the first fruit of the Spirit is love, we are assured that we see God's love in us and we are thereby assured that we possess the Holy Spirit and are therefore indwelt by God. Similarly since the Spirit is the Spirit of truth the fact that we are enabled to confess Jesus as the Son of God and Saviour of the world is another evidence of God abiding in us by his Spirit, and of our abiding in him. 'Whoever confesses that Jesus is the Son of God, God abides in him,' because that confession comes from the Holy Spirit who is the Spirit of truth. So we come to verse sixteen and the evidence of abiding in love. We know and believe the love God has for us, then he goes on, 'God is love and he who abides in love abides in God and God abides in him'. There are three things in that verse about our relation to the love of God, and they are all related to the ministry of the Holy Spirit. We know the love of God. We believe the love of God. And we abide in the love of God. The first two are really the Spirit's ministry of persuading us of God's love. We then need to bask in it and to take it in the wonder of God's love for us. It matters to God about you.

That leads us on to the theme of love perfected in us (vv. 17–21). The two marks of love being perfected in us is our attitude God-ward and our attitude man-ward.

The God-ward attitude is confidence rather than fear, and it is particularly confidence for the day of judgement. This word 'confidence' is one of the characteristic words of John's epistle. Literally, it means, freedom of speech. Not just with our boldness at the throne of judgement. The point is that clothed in Christ's righteousness we have something to say on the day of judgement (v. 17). What does that mean? Even though we are still in this world, we are looked upon by the Father with the same acceptance with which he looks upon Christ. Says R. C. H. Lensky, 'It is an incredible truth, that when God the Father looks upon us even now in this world, he sees us as though he were looking on Christ.' So on the day of judgement we are going to have freedom of speech, not because of anything that there is in us or anything we have done, but because God has dealt with us as he has dealt with his Son. There is no fear in love, for fear has to do with punishment (v. 18). That is the God-ward attitude. It is confidence rather than fear. The man-ward attitude is love rather than hatred. 'We love because he first loved us' (v. 19). (The A.V. has, 'We love him', but there is no 'him' in the Greek, and the R.S.V. is correct to omit it.) The point is that love is born in our hearts and becomes a possibility for us only because God has taken the initiative and loved us. And John applies it to the whole question of loving our brother. And with this devastating piece of logic he thrusts the point home, 'He who does not love his brother whom he has seen he cannot love God whom he has not seen.' You can tell whether and how much a man loves God by the way he treats his brother.

In chapter five we meet again the tests of belief, of love and of obedience (vv. 1–5). The test of belief opens and closes these first five verses. In verse one it means that faith is the evidence of the new birth. And that's an important thing to grasp. Faith is not the cause of the new birth, but the evidence of it, as the tenses here make abundantly plain. Literally, it is everyone who is believing, the present tense, has been begotten of God, the past tense. And John is careful to point out that believing is a result of the new birth, not the cause of it. From that point he goes on to the test of love. 'Everyone who loves the Father, loves his child as well,' as the New International Version puts it. In verse two he puts this the other way round and weaves in the third test of obedience. (In these five verses faith or belief, love, and obedience or obeying his commandments, come in all the way through.) 'By this we know that we love the children of God when we love God and obey his commandments.' In other words, we can test our love for God both by our love for one another and by our obedience to him; loving God and keeping his commandments are interwoven. Professor F. F. Bruce helpfully says, 'Love to God and obedience to God are so completely involved in each other that anyone of them implies the other too.' And on this central test of obeying God's commandments John has a word of encouragement and hope in verse three. The great tendency of human nature, when we are faced with this test is to regard the commandments of God, perhaps not publicly but secretly, as irksome and repressive. Whereas the will of God is good and acceptable and perfect for his children is the reason God's commandments are not grievous. One is because of God's eternal nature and the other is because of our redeemed nature. His commandments are not burdensome, his will for his creatures is all wise and all loving and all perfect (v. 3).

Studies in the First Epistle

'This is the victory that overcomes the world even our faith' (v. 4). It is the world and its ways that makes the commandments of God a burden, but the world and every other power which would militate against our obedience to the commandments of God has been overcome by our birth from God. God has given us a nature which will delight in keeping his commandments and have the power to overcome so as to obey them. That is the distinctive thing about God's commandments and about the whole Christian ethic.

In verses six to twelve we have the ground of assurance. Here we come to a notoriously difficult passage. 'This is he who came by water and blood.' First, let me just point out that it has a purpose. It is to demonstrate the grounds on which we believe in Jesus and have assurance concerning him. 'He who came' is almost a technical term in John's writings used mostly in the gospel for the Messiah. And I want to say to you without going into the pros and cons that I take the water and the blood to refer to Jesus' baptism and his death. When it is said that Jesus came by water and blood, I suggest that in these two places he entered upon and fulfilled his Messianic ministry. At his baptism Jesus publicly consecrated himself to the task of being a sin-bearer, and the Spirit was bestowed upon him without measure for the accomplishment of this task. However, he came 'by blood' also, and this was what the heretics (of whom John is writing) denied. The Apostles affirmed that he who was baptised by John the Baptist in Jordan, and he whose life-blood was shed on Calvary is the same Jesus, the same Christ. In other words, John is affirming that Jesus both took our nature and bore our sins. The one is affirmed at his baptism, the other is accomplished at his death. His baptism was therefore the initial act and his death the consumating act of his self consecration to the work of redemption. So John speaks of him as he who came not with water only, but with the water and the blood. Now what the heretics were denying was that the same Jesus who was here in the flesh could possibly have been God's instrument for the world's redemption. But the Apostle confirms that the two are brought together, and the Holy Spirit's witness to the divine-human person and saving work of Jesus, is probably a reference to that inward witness of the Holy Spirit (v. 7). (The A.V. includes additional material in verse seven which is from the Vulgate and not the Greek, and every modern translation properly omits it.) In verse eight you have the three witnessing together, the water and the blood and the Spirit, and it seems that this is the combination of the objective and subjective witnesses to the life and death of Jesus. These witnesses are, in fact, God's testimony to his Son. His perfect life taking on human nature, his saving death and the confirming ministry of the Holy Spirit. But there is still another testimony and that's the inner testimony of the Spirit or the testimony of experience if you like. 'He who believes in the Son of God has the testimony in himself' (v. 10). This is an additional testimony. When we believe God gives us the testimony in ourselves, a subjective personal testimony of experience. While it is not the ground of our assurance it is a confirmation of it.

Verses eleven and twelve describe the substance of this testimony God has given. 'This is the testimony that God gave us eternal life and this life is in his Son.' It concerns what God has given us, how he has given it and how we may have it. What he has given us is eternal life, and the nature of that life Jesus defined for

Studies in the First Epistle

us as fellowship with God through Christ. How he has given it is in his Son. That is, you cannot have eternal life without having Christ. Eternal life, therefore, is not a thing but a person, and it is exclusively found in Christ. How we may have eternal life is, therefore, obvious. We may have it by having him, 'He who has the Son has life.' This leads on to verse thirteen where John gathers together the great purpose of his writing, 'That they might know that they have eternal life'. That is that they might have assurance. There is an important link which we should notice. Many people imagine that it is presumption to be sure that you are a Christian, almost as if you are making some kind of boast. But what John wants us to be sure of is not anything to do with boasting in ourselves, but that we possess eternal life. That is that we have Christ and that we are related to him. We are simply relying on God's testimony in his word. When we fill in a form that includes the question 'Are you married or single?', we don't reply 'That's not for me to say'. Of course it's for us to say. What we are saying is not, 'I am the best husband there ever has been,' or 'the best wife there ever has been'. What we are asked is, do you have a husband or do you not? And when we ask, 'Are you a Christian' we are asking, 'Do you have a Saviour or do you not?' Have you believed the testimony, are you relying on God's word and promise? This is the testimony of this letter.

In verses fourteen to seventeen John moves naturally into one particular area where Christian assurance leads to Christian confidence and that is in prayer. This word confidence comes yet again as 'freedom of speech'. John twice refers to boldness before the throne of judgement (2:28 and 4:17) and twice to boldness before the throne of grace (3:21 and 5:14). But there are certain things we need to learn about true prayer from these verses. First, this confidence is in him, not in prayer. Secondly, this confidence is in his perfect will. It is not getting God to do my will, but coming to him that his will may be done. This confidence, thirdly, is in God's hearing and in our having (v. 15). Not just that God hears us, but that God gives us the answer. Having dealt with prayer in general, John proceeds in verse sixteen to speak in particular about intercession for an erring brother. The primary lesson of this verse is that it contains this urgent appeal to pray for an erring brother. When a man is found in sin, the first reaction of a Christian brother is not that he will be censorious towards him, but that he will pray for him.

What is the 'sin unto death?' (v. 16). There are three ways in which the word *death* is used in the New Testament. One is physical death, the separation of the soul from the body. The second is spiritual death, the separation of the soul from God. And the third is eternal death, the separation of soul and body from God forever. Two questions are raised here. 1. With what sort of death is John associating this sin? 2. To whom is he referring as a brother? In my opinion the answer to the second question is that he is probably not speaking about a believing brother, because he does use the word in a much more general sense elsewhere. The answer to the first question seems to me that it would be difficult to say physical death, because as far as we know, no list of sins exists in the New Testament for which physical death is the inevitable outcome. There are some like Ananias and Sapphira, but no general list. Also it would be difficult to say spiritual death because the wages of all sin is death, and John is speaking about

Studies in the First Epistle

a special sin. It must therefore be eternal death. And there is such a sin for which Jesus says there is no forgiveness either in this world or the world to come. 'I tell you every sin and blasphemy will be forgiven men, but the blasphemy against the Spirit will not be forgiven' (Mat. 12:31). For such sin, John says, I do not say pray because as there is no forgiveness for such a sin there is no point in praying for forgiveness. But let me say that this sin against the Holy Spirit is the sin of ascribing the works of Jesus to the devil and of the devil to Jesus. It is the state of final hardness of heart which calls good evil, and evil good. Needless to say, the one person who certainly has never committed that sin is the person who is worried that he has done so.

Finally to John's last three affirmations. First, we know that come what may the believer is secure. We know that anyone born of God does not sin and he who was born of God that is Christ, God keeps him and the evil one does not touch him. That is the first clarion call of assurance (v. 18). Second, we know that the alternative to being the Lord's is to be under the tyranny of the evil one. We know that we are of God and the whole world is in the power of the evil one (v. 19). Finally, we know that we know God. This is what Christ has done for us. He has brought us to know God and in the end of the day that is all that matters in the world (v. 20).

A SINGLE, STEADY AIM

Four studies in the Book of Nehemiah by the Revd. J. Alec Motyer, M.A., B.D.

1. Beginning: Getting the Foundations Right (Nehemiah 1:1 – 3:32)

Nehemiah comes before us in the Bible as the man who began, continued and ended. He set his hand to the work of God and he brought that work of God right through to the end. That is the story line on which Nehemiah bases his testimony.

The vision of the need dawned upon Nehemiah and seemed to be impressed upon his heart (1:3) by the Spirit of God. And he persevered in considering the possibility that this was the work of God for him so he carries the matter over from vision to inception (2:17). He then continues in the work of perseverance and records in his diary the work half done (4:6). A further progress report comes in chapter six verse one. Finally, the completion (6:15) quietly recorded, 'The wall was finished'.

The book of Nehemiah speaks to us at every point where we are 'stop-go' Christians, or more accurately 'go-stop' Christians. At every point whether we consider building ourselves up in our most holy faith, or whether we consider the building up of the Church of

God, the book of Nehemiah speaks to us because it tells of a man who set his hand to a building task and brought that task to completion. So often the tale of our own inner life is of an attempt to lay a foundation and a failure to build, of something attempted and nothing accomplished.

In his book there are three stages:

1. Beginning: Getting the foundations right. 'Laying the foundations' – how it all began (1:1–3:32). There must be a way of laying foundations which is in itself something of a guarantee that the work will be carried through to completion.

2. Persevering: Stress-points and Strong-points (4:1–6:19). A key expression is 'It came to pass when Sanballat heard that we had builded the wall that he was angry' (v. 1). But Nehemiah perseveres until he can say that the work is finished.

3. Living: The Citizen's Chapter (7:1–9:38) and The Enemy Within (10:1–13:31). It's one thing to build a wall, it's another thing to build a community.

The first question is: How are foundations laid? Is there some way of making a beginning, which is so well done and so securely established, that will guarantee it going to go through to the end? In the first three chapters we find four principles of foundation-laying. First is the 'principle of individuality'. The importance of the individual who sees clearly the call of God, to test it out until he is certain that it is real. For example Nehemiah records, 'I asked them concerning the Judeans' (v. 1). They didn't come and tell him. They came back with the news but with no concern to share the news so Nehemiah asked them concerning the Judeans and Jerusalem.

Over a hundred years before Nehemiah (586 B.C.) Jerusalem had been torn asunder by the Babylonians

Studies in the Book of Nehemiah

and the people of God had been taken away to captivity in Babylon. Between the years 586 and 539 the Persian empire succeeded the Babylonian empire, and the first emperor, Cyrus, decided that all captives in his empire should be restored, if they wished, to their original homelands.

The book of Ezra (1–6) records how the first company of returning captives, a small company compared with the total people in exile, came back to Jerusalem (539 or 538 B.C.). The next news that we have of that returned community is in the time of Ezra when he returned to Jerusalem on a spiritual mission as an accredited teacher of the law of Moses. It seems very likely that some of the enthusiasm engendered by Ezra's visit (458 B.C.) rubbed off in a political or nationalistic direction. But it began to flow out into an unauthorised rebuilding of the walls of Jerusalem and some of their enemies reported this to the emperor, Artaxerxes, who commanded that the building should cease. These enemies went to Jerusalem with the royal mandate causing the work to cease and tearing down the walls of Jerusalem. It's very likely the news of that action came to Nehemiah. The ruination of the city of God and the reproach of the people of God took hold of this man and it became his personal responsibility. At the start of the book of Nehemiah there is this principle of the individual being gripped by concern for the work of God and hearing the call of God. But the individual is always plus God who reassures with the promise, 'Surely, I will be with you.' However, individual responsibility can so easily become an irresponsible individualism, and we can run off on what is no more than a personal whim. So we move on from the principle of individuality, to the ways in which God sanctifies and controls individuality so that it does not become an unsanctified individualism.

The second principle of foundation-laying is this: Is there a way to begin which in itself guarantees that the work will carry forward to completion? Yes. It is the principle of prayer *(v. 4)*. As concern grips Nehemiah his reaction is to weep and mourn, but his counter-action is to pray. At once he begins to attack the problem, and he begins the attack in the place of prayer. And it was immediate. There was no gap between the hearing and the praying, and it was total. It was also an expression of a deep personal concern, 'I sat down and wept and mourned'. In English there is some distinction between 'moved' and being 'grieved'. The second word goes deeper than the first. He was not only moved by the picture of the plight of the people of God, but he was also grieved by it. It came home to him with the force of personal bereavement, for the word translated 'mourned' is used in the Old Testament in the context of bereavement. His prayer was continuous. The Hebrew verbs behind that translation are continuous verbs which means, 'I continued in fasting and prayer'. He locked himself into the position of intercession. In fasting Nehemiah detached himself from other preoccupations; which is the very heart of the Biblical idea of fasting. Detached from other claims and preoccupations in order to give priority and exclusive attention to the work of intercession. He prayed, that is to say, he verbalised his intercession. He didn't confuse the possession of a prayer list with the practice of prayer. He actually put it into words. And he prayed for three months (1:1 and 2:1). (The month Chis-leu was the ninth month of the year and the month Ni-san is the first month of the following year.) But it was God

Studies in the Book of Nehemiah

who kept him and held him in place of prayer (1:11). 'Prosper I pray thee thy servant, this day,' Nehemiah prayed the first day. And again the second day he said, 'O Lord, today.' For three to four months he went on saying, 'O Lord today.' And the Lord kept saying 'No.' It was God who kept him in the place of prayer. There is, however, much more here than the example of one man. There is also a message from God which is that if his work is to be founded in such a way that it will go through to the place of completion, it must have its foundation laid in the place of prayer.

Nehemiah is also noted for what are often called 'telegraph' prayers. How, in a second, he would shoot up a prayer to God. But Nehemiah's telegraphing a prayer to God is held in the context of a telephoning of prayer to God, whereby he is constantly in a place of prayer. Nehemiah gives us a sample of prayer (1:5 to 11), and it may help if we look at it in three sections. In the opening three verses his concentration is upon the nature of God. If we are to pray in the name of God then we must be clear about the God who bears that name. Then from verse eight to ten we have prayer finding its root in the word of God. That is to say if we are to pray effectively we must ask for those things which are according to the word of God. And in the last verse (v. 11) we have the third element which is prayer and the will of God.

Prayer must be rooted in the nature of God – we must ask things which are suitable to the divine character. In this prayer, Nehemiah first speaks to God in his own person. 'I beseech thee O Lord.' If you look at your Bible you will find that the four letters of the word LORD are capital letters. That means that it represents the divine name, 'Yahweh' or 'Jehovah'. The name by which God is known within his family and the name by which he is addressed by his intimates. Yahweh speaks of a God who saves his people and overthrows his enemies, as in the time of Exodus.

Secondly, Nehemiah speaks to the God of heaven. This title of the God of heaven is used four times in the book of Nehemiah, twice in this passage. Nehemiah is facing circumstances of great difficulty beyond unaided human power. When we face circumstances that are beyond human power, we address ourselves to the God who is supreme over all earthly circumstances, the God of Heaven.

Thirdly, prayer as addressed to God in his dignity. The two words 'great' and 'terrible', are not without significance. The word 'great' expresses the objective reality. Our God is a great God. And the word 'terrible' expresses a subjective sense, that he is so. The feeling of the greatness of God. Prayer arms us for the conflict of everyday, for the person who has been in the place of prayer has been in the place of true greatness, and the person who has been in the place of prayer has been in the place of true fearfulness. That person is then equipped to face any terror that the world may choose to face him with because it is nothing like the greatness and the terror that resides in his God.

Fourthly, God is addressed in his moral mercies (v. 5). He is a God who keeps covenant and mercy with them that love him and keep his commandments. There is that to which God has committed himself and those to whom God commits himself. So that in every situation however dreadful, the covenant stands, 'I am your God now, you are my child now'. He is a God who keeps covenant and mercy. The word is translated usually in the R.S.V. as 'steadfast love', and that captures it ex-

Studies in the Book of Nehemiah

actly. It is the undeviating love of God which he has pledged in his covenant. And here are those to whom he commits himself, 'Those who love him and keep his commandments'. The mercies of God are moral mercies. There is a subjective response of love towards God who loved us even unto the blood of the Lamb. And there is an objective response of obedience to his commandments.

Fifthly, Nehemiah addresses God in his loving and attentive concern with these words, 'Let thine ear be attentive' (v. 6). Again, it's a continuous verb. And this is the attention required, 'That thine ear may continue attentive, and thine eye continue opened.' He claims the attention of God because he prays for the children of God. This is the way in which prayer makes us aware of our privileged status. We can go to God and say, 'Lord hear us for Jesus sake.' We can also go to God and say, 'Lord, hear us for your promise sake.' But we can also go to God and say, 'Lord hear us for our sake because we are your servants.'

Sixthly, God is addressed in his holiness. Notice the way Nehemiah's prayer flows in an unbroken sequence into a confession of sin. Sin is corporate, 'we have sinned'. Sin is individual 'I have sinned'. And sin is progressive, 'and my Father's house hath sinned'. Ancestral sin in the Old Testament is never offered as an excuse for sin, but as a way of saying that man stands in a place of mounting guiltiness because he inherits the sinfulness of all that has gone before him. So Nehemiah confesses sin, and he discovers that sin is an offence against the person of God (v. 7). Sin offends God in his person, in his requirements, and in his mercies. Prayer exposes the reality of the situation, because the reality of the situation is not the broken down wall of Jerusalem. The reality of the situation is that sin in the people of God has destroyed the city of God. The city of Jerusalem fell because of the sins of Manassah. The whole of Bible history exists to tell us that history turns upon the hinge of sinfulness not upon the hinge of politics. And Nehemiah brings the opening part of his prayer to this conclusion, he comes into the place of confession. He has rehearsed the whole of the nature of God as he knows that nature, and the nature of God brings him into the place of confession.

He then moves on to prayer and the word of God. Prayer must be rooted in God's promises. I come into the place of prayer on the basis of something that God has said. And he recounts the experience of Moses and the Israelites, and he cites two distinct things. To return, that is the practice of repentance. To keep God's commandments, that is to accept the law of God as the rule of life. The result is an irresistible regathering and a total reconciliation. And as Nehemiah proceeds with this (v. 10) he establishes, scripturally, the claim of the people of God to those mercies. It's not only that such are the promised mercies, but these are the people who have a right to them. So he prays along the line of the word of God, and he brings his prayer to a conclusion (v. 11) in relation to the will of God. That is the centrepiece of this study, laying foundations. According to the will of God foundations must be laid in the place of prayer.

Finally, chapter two contains two more foundation principles. The principle of divine leadership (vv. 1–10) and association (2:11–3:32), that is, to establish the fellowship through which the vision is to be realised. Nehemiah says that he prayed 'This day', and that 'I was the king's cupbearer'. He tells us that in order to

Studies in the Book of Nehemiah

indicate that he not only wanted to get things moving straight away, but he was in daily opportunity to do so. So both the desire and the opportunity were there together. But desire and opportunity in themselves do not constitute obedience. He must wait for God. And so we read, 'It came to pass in the month of Nisan, in the twentieth year of King Artaxerxes when wine was before him, I took up the wine and gave it to the king. Now I had not been beforetime sad in his presence.' I'm not certain that he was sad in his presence then. In the A.V. the word 'beforetime' is in italics which means it's not in the Hebrew. Nehemiah was saying, 'As far as I knew I was carrying no heaviness of spirit at that moment, I was carrying no visible heaviness of countenance. And the king said to me "Why is your countenance sad, seeing you're not sick?".' God, unknown to Nehemiah, had printed concern upon his face. The king added, 'This is nothing else but sorrow of heart,' meaning malice of forethought, or some hidden evil design against the king's welfare. 'Then Nehemiah was very sore afraid.' He feared for his life and for the whole future of the vision that God had given him. He must speak straight away. Let him hesitate now and the king will be confirmed in his suspicion.' So he said, 'Let the king live forever. Why should not my face be sad when the city the place of my father's sepulchre lies waste?' There it is, out in the open at last. And when the king invited Nehemiah's request, he prayed to the God of heaven. God who gave the opportunity and the words, also gave the boldness (v. 7) so that he went on to capitalise on the situation. He asked for letters of authority to the governors and a letter of mandate to Asaph, the king's forester, for timber and equipment. And God gave success (v. 7–9). The king even sent with him captains of the army and horsemen. How abundantly worthwhile it was to wait until the moment God came. Nehemiah had to discipline and sanctify individuality in the place of prayer and by honouring the principle of divine leadership.

To conclude this first Bible study, the principle of association. In other words, to establish the fellowship through which the vision will be realised, because though the vision is individually granted the fulfilment is corporately achieved. Nehemiah, the individual, sees the building of a wall but it is going to take the whole of a united company to deal with it. However, in chapter two we notice that there is a fellowship to be excluded, and a fellowship to be cherished. Sanballat and company must be cut out as Nehemiah says, 'But you have no portion nor right nor memorial in Jerusalem.' That is to say, you have no claim that would stand up to examination, you have no memorial, you have never done anything here that would justify us in accepting you now. There is a fellowship that has to be cut out, and there is a fellowship to be cherished. A shared concern, a shared testimony, a shared status and a shared commitment. Nehemiah enjoyed a wide variety of fellowship. The Tekoites who were not abashed when 'their nobles put not their necks to the work'. Shallum the wise man, who mobilised his daughters. Baruch who, it says, 'Earnestly repaired'. You can see him out there with his spectacles on, attending to every detail. And Binnui who undertook a second stint of building. Zadok who worked. Meshullam who only had a room, but he built the wall opposite his room. Priests, goldsmiths and apothecaries, all were there. They were there because they had a shared concern, a shared testimony, and a shared status and rank within the city of

God and they were all alike. They were all alike, committed to their work. The principle of association is individual commitment, waiting upon God, and a church in fellowship.

2. Persevering: Stress Points and Strong Points (Nehemiah 4:1 – 6:19)

No sooner does the work begin than the work is attacked. The work does not go unchallenged, it did not do so then, it never does and it never will until the people of God are safe in Glory. 'Sanballat heard that we builded the wall he was angry' (4:1). In a word, he heard and he hated. The two things happened together. The work of God is always opposed. The name at that time was Sanballat. There have been many names throughout the history, but there is one abiding name, the name of the arch enemy, Satan. Using many instruments but always himself *hearing* and *hating*.

Sanballat as we learn in the books of Ezra and Nehemiah, was the governor of the province of Samaria, the remainder of the old northern kingdom. And one can only presume that while Jerusalem lay in ruins he was quietly able to add the province of Juda to the province of Samaria. It would certainly seem to be an adequate explanation of his incessant opposition to the rebuilding of Jerusalem, that he was his own authority and his own domain being threatened and eroded. And

Gathering together . . .

Visitors from overseas and Harry Sutton

(*Top*) Eric Alexander gives the morning Bible study
(*Middle and bottom*) Youth meetings

(*Top*) Children's programme
(*Bottom*) Tim Buckley leads an open air meeting in the market square

he was unwilling to yield up one inch of territory on which he could exert a claim whether right or wrong. He was moved by jealousy for his own authority. And here is the onset of opposition in a speech full of scorn born of animosity. It would appear that Sanballat was entertaining a visiting head of State, Tobiah, the provincial governor of Ammon. And Sanballat chose this occasion to start the campaign of opposition to the building of the wall. He attacks, first of all, the people of God. He attacks them in their own person, 'What do these feeble Judeans?' Secondly, he attacks them in their hopes, 'Will they restore or regather?' It was the hope of the people of God to restore the ancient Jerusalem. He mocks their hopes. 'Will they sacrifice?' He mocks their religious confidence in God. The testimony of Nehemiah had obviously not gone unheard. Addressing Sanballat, Nehemiah had said: 'The God of heaven, he will prosper us' (2:20). In the way the Hebrew is set out there those words stand in the emphatic place, so that what Nehemiah said to Sanballat was really equivalent to this. 'There is a God of heaven, he will prosper us, that's where we stand, that's where we start.' He mocks their enthusiasm. They have been busy as beavers upon the work of God, as though if you started in the morning you would finish it at night. He mocks their problems. 'Will they revive the stones out of the heaps of rubbish, seeing that they are burnt?' And Tobiah in responding to this speech of welcome adds his own touch, 'Why not leave it to the jackals, they will be prowling round at night and all it needs is one of them to walk around the wall and that will solve the problem.' And there is mockery of the people of God.

As we read on we discover that the advancing work

meets with mounting opposition. When Sanballat, Tobiah, the Arabians, the Ammonites and the Ashdodites heard that Nehemiah and party were repairing the walls they were very angry (v. 7). The work is advancing and the opposition is increasing. The very interesting comparison between verse six and verse eight. In verse six it says, 'We built the wall and all the wall is joined together.' Let me use the word 'bonded'. All the wall was bonded together. The various portions of the wall were beginning to link up. The wall was bonded together. In verse eight, they are all bonded together. The enemies are being bonded together in a ring, they are around the people of God. If they would mock the enthusiasm of the Judeans, they have a great enthusiasm of their own, as verse eleven tells us. So we learn that the work of God is always under attack and that this attack has a nagging deliberating pressure upon the people of God. So in verse ten, Judah said, 'The strength of the bearers of burdens has faultered and there is much rubbish and we are not able to build the wall.' There is a voice that says we cannot go on, our strength is at an end, the difficulties are insurmountable, we cannot go on. Resources too small, problems too great. That sounds very modern, but it comes from the year 445 B.C.

Verse twelve is a very difficult verse to translate and there will be as many different translations as there are different versions of the Bible. But it would seem that the Revised Standard Version or the Revised Version offer the two most likely possibilities. The R.S.V. says, 'Of all places where they live they will come up against us.' Here is a voice which says you had better stop the work now for if you don't they will stop it for us. Or alternatively, in the R.V. you have the picture of people

Studies in the Book of Nehemiah

coming into Jerusalem from outside. We know from later on in the chapter that this was happening. They were coming to work and to visit workers. People coming in from immediate contact with the outposts of the surrounding enemy and as they came in from every place so they said it over and over again, ten times said Nehemiah. So if verse ten tells us there is a voice which says we cannot go on, verse twelve says there is a voice which says we must go back. The first is the voice of self-pity, it's too much for me. And the second is the voice of self-advantage, I've got to look after myself. Pressure of the enemy erodes the spirit of the people of God, but the chapter which tells us that the work of God is always attacked also tells us that the resources are sufficient.

The resources of the people of God are: 1. Prayer. The first counter-attack against the enemy (vv. 4, 9 and 15). And what a remarkable prayer it was that Nehemiah prayed. It seems to have as much hatred in it as was expressed against him by others. Would you ever pray concerning anybody that their reproach would be turned back upon their own head and that their iniquity would not be forgiven or their sin covered? They are fighting words. But the first thing about this prayer is that it is based on confidence that God is as one with his people. 'Hear O our God; for we are despised' (v. 4). Why is God to hear? Because of something that is true about us, we are despised. Why are you to hear us? Because they have offended you (v. 5). They have offended us and they have offended you, and we are bound together. What a marvellous thing, God identified with his people. When the people of God are hurt, God is offended. The second thing about Nehemiah's prayer is that it is Biblical and expresses the Biblical truth of divine recompense. The Bible straightly warns the people of God never to take vengeance. 'Vengeance belongs to me, saith the Lord.'

There are two Biblical truths enshrined in Nehemiah's prayer. The first is this: If someone makes a false accusation against somebody else and before the courts it is proved to be false, malicious accusation, the false accuser is to suffer in himself that penalty which he would have brought upon the other person (Deuteronomy 19:18, 19). That is what Nehemiah prays here. In answer to the accusation, 'we are despised', he prays, 'turn back their reproach upon their own head, let them be given up to spoiling in a land of captivity'. Our work is to bring back the people of God from captivity. If God is provoked, the Scripture would say, there can be no forgiveness of sins. So he is praying what the Bible allows him to pray. His prayer is based on Bible doctrine, and he is doing what we shudder and hesitate to do, expressing his prayer with realism. We would be quite happy if Nehemiah had said in his prayer, 'O Lord, please deal with them.' But if we were to ask Scripture how would God deal with them, we would discover that God deals with the false accuser by bringing his accusation back on his own head, and God deals with the person who provokes his holiness by refusing to forgive his sin. Nehemiah simply takes the Bible literally and expresses his prayer with realism. Tell me, would you ever pray concerning the unconverted, 'O, Lord, I beseech you in flaming fire, take vengeance upon those who know not the Lord Jesus Christ and who obey not the Gospel and confine them to an eternal punishment apart from yourself'? Would you ever pray that prayer? But you do, every time you pray, 'Even so come Lord Jesus.' That is the realistic opposite side to the glory of the Second Coming. That is what will happen. Prayer is the resource of the people of God against all the power of the enemy.

Their second resource is, consecrated work (v. 6). Many versions have, 'So we built the wall.' But the Hebrew particle there is simply connective, 'And we built the wall.' We prayed and we built. Part of their counter-attack was to go on with the work of God. It was a consecrated work, the people had a mind. The Hebrew says that they had a heart for the work, their heart was in the work of God. We often wait for God to give us victory, so as to liberate us to do his work. Whereas the work of God is part of the way of victory. Use the book of Nehemiah as a great visual aid. You build a wall and you have the victory. The heart in the task is an element of the Biblical doctrine of living a victorious life.

Thirdly, ceaseless vigilance (vv. 9 and 13). 'We set a watch against them because of them.' The enemy is ceaselessly ready to attack, therefore there must be a ceaseless vigilance. And that vigilance must be concentrated at the points that are most vulnerable, the exposed places.

Fourthly, a clear vision of God (v. 14). Nehemiah had a great message of encouragement. Remember the Lord, he is great, he is awesome. We also should have a message of encouragement for the people of God and the encouragement is to see God himself. Show them what God is like. The word 'Lord' in this verse equals Jehovah, Sovereign. One who in himself is of sovereign authority and of sovereign executive power and against all the force of the enemy.

Fifthly, for victory. 'Fight for your brethren, your sons and your daughters, your wives and your houses'

(v. 14). A responsible involvement and an acceptance of individual responsibility for the welfare of the people of God. And so they came to victory (v. 15). The threat was over. The victory had been won.

In chapter five we come to a second element of assault. A specific assault upon unity and fellowship. Where fellowship is attacked the community and the individual are at risk. In the previous chapter Nehemiah dealt with the collective strength of the people of God. Nehemiah holds the people together, in the bonds of community, in the bonds of religion, in the bonds of love (brethren, sons, daughters, wives and households) (4:14). He then proceeds to organise that unity into a collective strength where the attack is (vv. 19, 20). This leads to chapter five where there are three aspects of economic stress. First in verse two. Here are people with large families who are foregoing their wages for two months and they say, 'We haven't enough left to buy food, let us get corn that we may eat.' At the end of verse three 'because of the dearth'. It was a time of economic stress because there was a famine, and two things were happening. Some said they were mortgaging their fields, vineyards and houses to get corn because of the dearth. Their assets were gradually passing into the hands of the finance houses. In verse four, there was the Inland Revenue, 'The King's tribute'. The inflationary situation brought about by the famine had hit them hard, and they had to borrow money to pay the land tax. So there was economic stress running right through the community. And in this economic stress brother was against brother. Brother was feasting upon the flesh of brother and division was coming into the people of God. Here is a classical division between the 'haves' and the 'have-nots'. Suppose there was an assault upon the city and it happens to fall upon the rich quarter. The poor people, who have been suffering at the hands of the wealthy money-lenders would say to themselves, 'Let them get on with it.' And the whole city falls, not just the wealthy quarter. It's against safety when unity goes. Thirdly, it belies the fears of God (v. 9). That's a most interesting thing because the sin, if you wish to put it this way, was against the second table of the law. That table of the law which teaches good neighbourliness. But Nehemiah appeals to the first table of the law, 'You are not fearing God'. If you have a proper fear of God in your heart you will have a proper reverence for the people of God in your life. It is contrary to the fear of God when unity suffers. Fourthly, it mars testimony (v. 9). It brings reproach. Fifthly, it is life below the highest. (Incidentally, how Nehemiah dealt with this dispute provides a thumbnail sketch for church leaders on how to deal with disunity in their churches.) The chapter ends with a striking testimony given by Nehemiah himself. He testifies that he surrendered his rights as governor (vv. 14, 15) and his opportunities (v. 16). Doubtless, sitting at the centre of administration he heard of many a bargain but he never took advantage of it. He didn't buy any land for his own advantage. He surrendered his rights, his opportunities and his resources (vv. 17, 18). He gives us two reasons. He feared God (v. 15) and he loved the people of God (v. 18). He gave an example of how to live within, and contribute to, a united people. Unity always fractures at the point of self-will and self-interest. Nehemiah said, 'I surrendered my rights, I surrendered my opportunities, I surrendered my resources, because only in that way could I express my fear of God and my concern for the welfare of God's people.'

And chapter six contains the third element of assault upon the people of God. First, work. Second, unity. Third, the individual. And the key words which describe this chapter come in verse two. 'Sanballat and Geshem sent unto me.' Sanballat and me. That is what this chapter is about. Sanballat has assaulted the work and he has been repulsed by God. The arch enemy has assaulted unity and he has been repulsed by the recovery of the Biblical standards of oneness and concern. The enemy now attacks the individual. The city will be as strong as any individual. That could be the way in. Nehemiah is attacked at the level of consecration (vv. 1–4). Notice how every advance is counter-attacked by the enemy. The enemy never gives up. The walls are now complete all that remains is the gates. Whether they meant to assassinate Nehemiah, or in some other way exert pressure upon him such as would withdraw his leadership from the people of God, we don't know. But they meant to do him a mischief. What is interesting is the way he replied 'I sent messengers to them saying I am doing a great work so that I cannot come down; why should the work cease while I leave it and come down to you?' (v. 3). He replied in terms of consecrated obedience. As long as we obey God, Satan cannot trip us up.

Secondly, Nehemiah is attacked at the level of reputation (v. 5). Sanballat sent an open letter. That is to say, something that anybody could read in which was written 'and Gashmu saith it'. Who is Gashmu? I know what your Bible has done, it has changed it to Geshem and I am not going to take the responsibility. Who is Gashmu? There is no such person. Sanballat wants to give the impression that there is a big rumour to this effect, everybody says it. Gashmu says it, what more would you want than that? He is bringing the pressure

Studies in the Book of Nehemiah

of rumour to bear upon Nehemiah. And what is Gashmu saying forsooth? That Nehemiah and the Judeans are planning to rebel for which cause they build the wall, and he would be their king. He is challenged at the point of reputation. But how does he reply? 'There are no such things done as thou sayest, but thou feignest them out of thine own heart' (v. 8). The beauty of an absolutely clear conscience. What a protection against inuendo, against the assault and fear of the enemy. Nehemiah was attacked at the level of reputation and he replied on the level of holiness.

And thirdly, he was attacked at the level of discernment (vv. 10–13). Shamaiah was under restraint and Nehemiah went to see him and he was met with this apparent word of God, 'Let us meet together in the house of God, within the temple'. An apparent message from God. 'A prophesy' Nehemiah later calls it. Surely the man of God must always listen to a prophesy. But this is how he replies. You tell me to go into the sanctuary to save my life, a man like me in there? Only the priest is in there. Remember King Hosiah? Did he go into the sanctuary with impunity, usurping the priest's office. Shall I go in there? says Nehemiah. What is he doing? He is comparing the pretended word of God with the actual word of God. He is not taking a naïve view of everybody who says, 'I'm a prophet. I'm speaking to you from God.' We have a veritable and proved word of God. By it, let us test all things. He is tested at the point of discernment, and he is a discerning believer because he knows the word of God. A clear-headed knowledge of Holy Scripture.

So the wall was finished. It was finished because it was well-founded and because in the midst of opposition they knew how to go on with God. They laid hold upon those means of grace, prayer, work, and the knowledge of God. The wall was completed because when fellowship was threatened fellowship was maintained. And the wall was completed because when the individual was attacked he replied to the attacks in terms of obedience and holiness and a knowledge of Holy Scripture. And the wall was finished.

3. Living: The Citizen's Charter (Nehemiah 7:1 – 9:38)

'So the wall was finished' (6:15). Chapter six verse fifteen draws a line across the story. Up to this point we have been pre-occupied with the work of building the wall. However, Nehemiah quietly reminds us that though the wall is finished the danger remains (vv. 15 to 19). There was a fifth column already in the midst of the city. Chapter seven verse one to three continues that theme of danger, the wall has been built but vigilance must not be relaxed. At this point Nehemiah rather delightfully takes us inside his own thinking and tells us that he is so thrilled with this new city that has come into being under his hand. The city was wide and large (v. 4).

Then there is the question of who is going to live there. 'My God put into my heart to gather together the nobles and the people that they may be reckoned by genealogy' (v. 5). The thought has come to him that here is a fresh work from the hand of God, here is the city of God. 'I want people living there who are special and as fresh as the city itself to occupy it.' And he begins to search the records. The records are recorded in a long list of names in chapter seven.

He is planning for the future population of the city but in the meantime the characteristic life of the city of God is beginning to take shape. I want you to notice that as soon as the wall was built it was marked pre-eminently by the reading of the word of God (8:1). And that reading of the word of God leads to a particular act of obedience, the keeping of the feast of tabernacles (v. 14). The reading of the word of God also brings about a season of national repentance and individual re-dedication (8:18 to 9).

First the introductions to a new theme (6:15). Up to this point Nehemiah's gaze has been consistently outward, to guard the city and the people of God from the assault of the enemy who was outside. But now a new topic is announced. Nehemiah turns his gaze inward. The city is now contained within its walls and Nehemiah begins to see how to order life within the city of God. We are no longer dealing with principles of building, we are turning to deal with principles of living. And the first of those principles comes at the beginning of chapter seven. It is a basic principle. It is so clear here, as indeed everything in the book of Nehemiah is clear, because the whole book is by way of an enormous visual aid so that we actually see. The enemy has not been banished by the building of the wall. Here then is a foundation principle of life for the people of God. There is no stage in the experience of the Church in this world which removes the need for vigilance. Either to the individual believer or to the whole company of believers. Vigilance must go on, so Nehemiah appointed gate-keepers. He gave his brother Hanani, and Hananiah, governor of the castle, charge over Jerusalem 'For he was a faithful man' (v. 2). Here is a contrast between the nobles to whom he has eluded at the end of chapter six. He was in the category of a faithful man. A man who could be trusted and who feared God above many. The sense of the awesomeness of God as felt by the people of God is one of the striking things in Nehemiah's testimony. Here was a man who feared God and therefore he was safe to be put in charge of the work of God, because he would not watch the faces of men, he would watch the face of God.

In verse three, Nehemiah makes very strict regulations about when the gates are to be opened and when the gates are to be shut. Nothing is to be left to chance. I like the translation 'Let not the gates be opened while the sun is hot, and while they are standing at ease let them shut the doors.' Nehemiah is aware that they will make sensible arrangements about keeping the gates closed at night time but he is afraid that in the drowsy mid-afternoon they might be forgetful. In verse four he makes a whole rounded obligation for everybody to watch. At the end of verse three we see that Nehemiah was second to none when it came to being subtle. If a man will watch over anything he will watch over his own patch. Vigilance must go on. You must have gate-keepers, an officer in overall charge of the city, a faithful God-fearing man who will watch the face of God. You must have regulations about opening and shutting, a citizen guard. Everybody has got to be involved in watching. It means that even though the wall is built all the principles described in the early chapters must continue to operate. They all come over into this new experience, they are not left behind. The wall is built, but the enemy is still alive. No stage of experience takes away the need for vigilance.

The second principle of life is enshrined in this long list of names. The individual basis of membership. The city was wide and large, but the people were few. Nehemiah is not taking a census, he is registering claims. And he is going to go back by way of genealogy to see who has the right to membership. Who has a right to live in the city of God? Now this is going to be a matter of not at looking at people in bulk, but of weighing people individually. Nehemiah wanted to people his city with those who had a valid claim to membership. It is very interesting to notice how he wanted to decide the validity of a claim. He did not go back to Abraham. Instead he says 'I found the book of the genealogy of them which came up at first' (v. 5). That is to say, he found a list of people with a genuine individual commitment to the cause of God. Not a broad sweeping thing like their descent from Abraham. But within the descent from Abraham, those who were unwilling to settle down in the comfort of a life in the Persian empire. Those who were prepared to commit themselves and face hardship in order to get back into the city of God. The individual basis of membership who has the birthright, are the permitted ones. There are at least two other major things which could be said about the individual basis of membership. An assurance of divine approval, God approves who you are and what you are for his city. And evidence of practical consecration, the consecration of our goods to the cause of God.

The third principle of life in the city of God is rejoicing in the knowledge of God's word. The three things are recognition of the word of God, knowledge of that word, and there is joy in knowledge. Life in the city quickly got going. The wall was completed on the twenty-fifth day of the sixth month, and life began on the first day of the seventh month. So they just had time to collect their wits, wash their hands, change their dungarees for their best suits and they were away. At once life took a very significant shape. There was a book which held the foremost place in the life of the city of God. And their first communal act was to gather themselves together, as one man, in the broad place that was before the water gate. There Ezra, the scribe, was asked to bring the book of the law of Moses (8:1) to Israel. And that book caused the people to understand the law (v. 8). This was a book which began from the start to dominate the common life of the people of God, and began to exercise its claim upon all with understanding and prolonged attention. It was the mark of the holy days which were appointed by God. The first day of the seventh month was a holy day appointed in the law of God and it was marked by listening to the law of God (vv. 1, 2). The feast of tabernacles, one of the holy times appointed by God, and it was marked by hearing the law of God (v. 18). But in chapter nine we have an ordinary day which the people for their own purposes had made special and they marked the day by giving a quarter of their time to listening to the word of God. If we can glance forward to chapter twelve verse twenty-seven we come to another special day, special because the people set it aside and how did they mark the day? 'On that day they read in the book of Moses in the audience of the people.' (13:1). See how the book is beginning to sweep right through their lives. It is the thing which dominates them from the first, claims their repeated prolonged attention and begins to mark every significant happening in the city, whether nominated by God or nominated by man. The central idea of the feast of tabernacles was to remember the great acts of God for the wilderness generation. And that reminder was focused upon the reading of the law of God. In chapter nine the focus of attention was personal and national repentance and re-dedication. So a quarter of the day is given to the reading of the word of God. No matter what the purpose, whether it was to remind them of God, to bring themselves into a new stage of spiritual experience, or to exalt their hearts in thanksgiving, the word of God was at the centre of their communal life.

Now let us see how that book is described. (i) It is described as to its origin (8:1). It is the law which the Lord gave, the origin is in God. (ii) It is described as to its communication (8:3). It was taught by the Spirit and given through Moses, so it has a double communication. The Spirit of God as the teacher, and Moses as the mediator. (iii) It is described as to its form. It is a book (8:7). (iv) Its content; what do you find when you read it? (8:4). You find law, commandments, statutes and judgements. (v) And it is described as to its recipients (9:3 and 10:29). It was given to Israel. Five things about the book. Its origin, transmission, form, content and recipients.

In this book of Nehemiah we have the setting that is true of Scripture. First its origin. Paul writes to Timothy, 'Every Scripture is inspired by God' (2 Tim. 3:16). But that does not quite catch the one word that is there in Greek. We can only catch that word by making up an English word, God 'breathed'. That is to say, it has its origin in God as his own breath.

Secondly, transmission. How aptly Peter sums up what we have found in Nehemiah, but in a clear doctrinal statement: 'No prophecy ever came by the will of man' (2 Peter 1:21). But there you have Nehemiah's double testimony. It was a book taught by the Spirit and given through Moses. And this is true of the whole prophetic Scripture, using the word 'prophecy' in its Biblical sense 'Of that which declares the wonderful works of God'. It came from God, and the human agents were taken and moved by the Spirit of God. Peter uses a word in his letter which is used at Paul's shipwreck (Acts 27), the ship being driven by a mighty wind. This was no ordinary or calm action of the Holy Spirit. This was not a gentle shove, but a howling gale of the Spirit of God as he took hold of his human agents and made them into men capable of bringing the word of God to the Church. Its transmission that has resulted in what we call verbal inspiration. That this word of man is the word of God. So Paul makes this calm claim: 'Which things also we speak, not in words which man's wisdom teaches, but which the Spirit teaches' (1 Cor. 2:13). The Holy Spirit so presiding over this whole process that it is not just the draft of Scripture but it is the very word in which the message is expressed. But how can a man become the vehicle of the word of God without losing his individuality and sacrificing his personality? Is it right that a man should be used as a mere typewriter? My reply would be that if God said to me, 'Would you mind if I used you as my typewriter?' I would say to him, 'Please feel free, I would be honoured.' I don't think that it is any derogation of man for him to be taken up and used in the purposes of God. And if God chose to use any man as a typewriter that would be a supreme dignity. But, in fact, it was not like that. There was no trespass upon the dignity of the human personality. Very often I find people who write about Biblical inspiration use an illustration of a stained glass window. They say that outside you have what we call the pure light of the sun. And that pure light strikes the stained glass window. On the other side you see no longer the pure light of the sun, but a light which has been tainted because it has come through an impure agent. And so there are those who say there is an inspiration of the word of God but we must remember that the Bible writers were ordinary men. Therefore, the pure word of God which left heaven untainted has come to us with the taints of fallen humanity. But think of the illustration in another way. In the best sort of stained glass window every colour, pattern, and figuration is there, because the designer so intended. He planned that window to bring pure sunlight into that place. Not an accident but a plan of the designer. In Jeremiah we read that the word of the Lord came saying, 'Before I formed you in the belly I knew you, before you came forth out of the womb I sanctified you. I have appointed you a prophet' (Jeremiah 1:5). You came to birth, not by any accident, not by the will of man, but by the purpose of God; to be in your day and generation, and for the Church as long as it will stay on earth, the stained glass window of my design. I made you what you are in order that you might bring the word of God to the people as a prophet moved by the Holy Ghost. The nearer a man comes to God the more he becomes a man, that's why Jesus is the perfect man. The nearer a man comes to God, the more he submits himself to the will of God, the more human he becomes. There is no devaluation of human personality in being perfectly conformed to the will of God. That is the definition of what a man is. A being made in the image of God. What we have in the Bible writers are men who are planned by God and who were so touched by God that they could be brought into this intimate communion with him

Studies in the Book of Nehemiah

which Jeremiah calls 'Standing in the fellowship of God' (chapter 23).

Our third word taken from Nehemiah is that we have 'a book'. It is deliberately planned in its content. It has a beginning, a middle, and an end. It is not subject to revision, subtraction, or alteration. It is there as a fixed entity (cf. Ezekiel 2:8 to 3:4). Ezekiel said it was written within and on the reverse side. In other words there was no room left for Ezekiel's own best thoughts. It was there in fixity, finality and completeness.

In the book of Nehemiah we find four words in which Nehemiah describes the content of the book. Law, commandments, statutes and judgement. The word 'law' is a particularly unfortunate translation. We can catch the feeling intended if we remember that in Proverbs we read such things as, 'My son hear the law of your father.' Law is instruction given by a loving parent to a beloved child. And it is in that way that God speaks to his people. He speaks to them as their teacher. Judgements, the word in English speaks of authority. The Judge on the bench making a pronouncement which brooks no contradiction. It means that God has made up his mind and has spoken. Statutes, the word is based on a verb which means, 'To engrave as on a rock'. When the word of God is called his statutes, it speaks of its abiding and unalterable character. It is graven in the rock for permanency. And Nehemiah's fourth word was commandments. That is its application to life. God takes his abiding principles and his eternal statement and brings them down for our obedience in the practical details of daily life.

Fifthly, and by no means of least importance, 'The word was given to Israel'. Given from God through men to the Church. It is directed primarily at the understanding. It was to be read before men and women and all who could hear with understanding (8:2), that was the qualification. The assumption is, of course, that adults can so hear, but how do you test whether to bring your family or not. Can they hear with understanding? (8:2). Chapter eight verse three at the end of the verse 'Men and women and those that could understand' (v. 3). 'They called the people to understand' (v. 7). 'They read the law of God distinctly and gave the sense so that the people understood the reading' (v. 12). It goes on and on to understand that is the response of the Church to the word of God. To understand what is there, to grasp it with the mind. In chapter eight there is a most interesting thing, from verse nine onwards. Nehemiah, Ezra and the Levites instructed the people: 'This day is holy unto the Lord your God, mourn not, nor weep. For all the people were mourning and weeping when they heard the word of the law.' That is to say that the words of the law were provoking an emotional reaction because they listened to its rebukes and gave themselves to an emotional response of weeping. And Nehemiah taught them to put their minds first, in relation to Holy Scripture. The joy of the Lord is your strength. It is a remarkable statement because they were weeping. The law had rebuked them. And Nehemiah said you can find joy in the God who rebukes. But what 'joy' was he talking about? He was talking about the joy of understanding the law of God.

Finally, the law of God led them to the spiritual experience of repentence (8:9). They wept when they heard the word. The law of the Lord leads individuals or in spiritual experience (8:12). The law of the Lord also led them into a life of obedience (8:14).

4. Living: The Enemy Within (Nehemiah 10:1 – 13:31)

The opening twenty-seven verses of chapter ten are the names of those who specifically signed a dedicatory covenant. It was a matter of individuals entering into a covenant with God, and they signed as representative of a whole people who wished individually to commit themselves to God. Here is the basic principle of this dedication (v. 28). They had understood what the book was saying, and they entered into a dedicatory promise to live according to that book. There were three matters which exercised them along the lines of obedience. Marriage (v. 30); the sabbath and the seventh year (v. 31) and the maintenance of the work of God (v. 32).

In chapter eleven Nehemiah expresses his desire to have a pure citizenry in the city of God. We have a list of the people brought in, with a further list in chapter twelve of the priests who participated in the original return before the time of Nehemiah. These two are virtually given over to these lists of names. From verse thirty-one we have a wonderful service, doubtless devised by Ezra and Nehemiah, in which two processions went around the walls of Jerusalem. The first was under Ezra, and the second under Nehemiah. They make their way around the circle of the wall as though claiming the wall for God. Then they come back and the two companies stand and give thanks in the courts of the house of God (v. 40). There are two matters related to that in verse forty-four and onwards. First, there is the appointment of the Levites, who will have charge of the house of God. And in the first three verses of chapter thirteen there is a further act of obedience to the word of God as it is read to them in the house of God. It concerns the purity of the people of God in the place of worship, those who can be included and those who can be excluded. The book concludes in chapter thirteen verse four onwards to verse thirty-one, where we learn something of the history of Nehemiah himself.

To give us the framework we should refresh our memories. In chapter two, verse six, at the time of Nehemiah's original interview with King Artaxerxes, the king and queen asked, 'How long will your journey be and when will you return?' It pleased the king to send Nehemiah and he set him a time. We later learn (5:14) that that time spread itself out to twelve years. Now the wall only took fifty-two days to build. It is hardly likely that when the King said to Nehemiah, 'How long will you be away?' that Nehemiah said, 'Well as a matter of fact, twelve years.' It is much more likely that he appointed a more modest time, but that when he made such a success of his work he was subsequently appointed governor and his governorship extended for twelve years. We do not know that, but this seems likely in terms of the story as told to us.

The material that lies before us for our study is in

Studies in the Book of Nehemiah

chapter nine. We face the reality that it's one thing to have the book and it's another thing to heed the book. We have already seen that the people of God are characteristically defined as the people under the authority of the book. The book was at the centre of their lives. In this chapter we have a review of the history of the people of God. They are drawing together what they have learned from the word of God, and as they review their history a revelation is made to them through the Holy Scriptures which leads them to the place of dedication. The truth of the word, leading to revelation of God, leading to dedication of God's people. This history begins with Abram, and the centrepiece is the righteousness of God (vv. 7, 8). In all his dealings with Abram this is what emerged. Election, regeneration, faith, covenant, the fidelity of God, and the righteousness of God. The next section is verses nine to twelve and the centrepiece of this little narrative is the self revelation of God to Israel in Egypt.

The next stopping place in the narrative is verse thirteen, Mount Sinai. God led his people by a straight and deliberate road from the land of Egypt to the mountain of Sinai. This was their immediate destination. 'Thou camest down upon Mount Sinai.' He brought them there to meet with him. Do you remember that dramatic verse in Exodus 19 when Moses brought the people out to meet God at Mount Sinai. And the centrepiece here is the revelation of the law of God as 'Right judgements, and true laws, and good statutes'. Right, true and good. Right because there was no admixture of anything that was bent, warped or misleading. True, because there was nothing in them that was false or erroneous. And good, because the whole administration of the law was beneficial and rich for the people of God. Through the eyes of the Pharisees we think of the law of God as an enormous burden. But remember that Jesus said that the Pharisees were a heretical set. In contrast the voice of the Old Testament is, 'O, how I love thy Lord, I find that it's right.' I find that it's true. I find that it's good. He brought the people to Mount Sinai in order that to the redeemed he might declare a pattern of life. That is the place of law in the Bible of God. Not a ladder for the unsaved to seek vainly to climb to glory, but a pattern of life for those who have been redeemed by the blood of the Lamb.

In verse fifteen, we come to the next stage of this review. Now sadness comes in. From Mount Sinai onwards, where they possessed the law, they persisted in breaking the law. No sooner had God spoken his word than they disobeyed. And he not only gave them food but he gave them leadership. 'The pillar of cloud by day, the pillar of fire by night' (v. 19). However, he not only attended to their ordinary daily wants of food and water, and leadership, but he went that step further. In verse twenty we read, 'Thou gavest them also thy Spirit'. The Holy Spirit of God with the people of God, as their teacher.

In verse twenty-two they come into the land and onwards to verse thirty they are in the land. The keynote here is the bounty of God. He brought them into a good and rich land and he showed himself to be a rich and bountiful God. The bounty of provisions (v. 25). The bounty of God in his care (v. 27). The bounty of truth (v. 30). From the second half of verse thirty to the end of the chapter the exile and the things which followed the exile.

The review enshrines a revelation, and now I want to draw out, what seems to me to be, the three main lines

Studies in the Book of Nehemiah

of revelation. They are the lines of sovereignty, compassion and sin.

Sovereignty, the greatness of God. It is on this note that the whole exercise of meditating upon the word of God begins. 'Thou, even thou, art Lord alone; thou hast made heaven, the heaven of heavens, with all their host, the earth, and all things that are therein, the seas, and all that is therein, and thou preservest them all; and the host of heaven worshippeth thee' (9:6). Notice how this verse will not allow us to evade the rigour of the sovereignty of God. If you could press right into the heart of all things the story would be the same. And if from the heart of things, the heaven of heavens, you press out to the circumference it is the same. There is nothing that he has not made. They are only there because the Creator holds them. This sovereignty theme runs right through the review. The characteristic verb which comes over and over again rather like a chiming bell in this review is the verb 'to give'. So that we get this feeling of the whole of life being suspended from the hand of a God who gives things in turn, and life is only lived upon earth because God gives it that shape or that capacity at that particular moment. First of all he is sovereign over political and natural forces (v. 10). In the Hebrew the verb 'gave' is used so that it reads, 'gave signs and wonders upon Pharaoh'. God also showed his sovereignty over all the natural forces at the Red Sea and demonstrated his sovereignty against the total power of Pharaoh. Political and natural forces subject to God. God gave 'right judgements'. He didn't ask their leave, he didn't say would you like the tables of the law. He was sovereign over his people (v. 13).

He was sovereign over all the resources of the earth, whether natural or supernatural. He is the giver of all.

He gave them bread from heaven (v. 15). He is sovereign in his freedom of self-giving for the benefit of his people (v. 20).

Then we read, 'Moreover thou gavest them kingdoms and peoples' (vv. 22, 24). God did not negotiate with Sihon king of the Amorites and Og the king of Bashan. He gave them to his people. He is sovereign over all the kings of the earth.

He is sovereign in his holy wrath, 'Thou gavest them into the hands of their adversaries' (v. 27). And he is sovereign in deliverance, 'Thou gavest them saviours' (v. 27). In verse thirty, we see him sovereign in punishment. So his sovereignty is not a theoretical thing but is the actual mode of the government of the world.

The second theme that we have in this revelatory meditation upon the word of God is the theme of compassion. First, a God ready to pardon (v. 17). The word there is the plural of the word 'forgiveness', a God of 'forgivenesses'. They are never exhausted because they are in the plural. God is gracious and full of compassion. (Compassion is the word in many translations.) According to thy manifold compassions *(v. 27)*. According to thy compassions (v. 31). The easiest way to understand that word compassion is to think of that marvellous story of Solomon and the two prostitutes *(*1 King's 3*)*. These two girls came with a case before Solomon, and this was deliberately selected by the Biblical historian in order to show the wonder of the wisdom that God had given to Solomon. You remember the story that one girl's baby died and she stole the other girl's baby and they brought this matter to the king to decide. He said, 'The matter is quite simple – let's have a sword and we'll cut the baby in two, and then you'll have half each.' And the girl who wasn't the mother agreed. But of the girl who was the mother we read 'her compassions were in turmoil'. And that is what the word compassion means. This whole internal compassionate involvement in the son of her womb. Indeed, the word 'compassion' is directly related to the word for a womb. And this is the motherly love of God for his people. A turmoil of passionate emotional involvement in the welfare of his people. And he is like that. He is a compassionate God. And it is a compassion which forbears (vv. 17, 19).

In verse seventeen they appoint a captain in order to return to Egypt. And in verse eighteen they make a golden calf to reject God himself. It says at the end of the verse 'They wrought great despite'. They offered a grave insult to God. But he is a God who is gracious and full of emotional turmoil of compassion. Forbearance. In verse twenty-seven it is the compassion which saves in answer to prayer. When he hears the cry of his people, it is just like that girl standing before Solomon, his emotions are in turmoil. A compassion which perseveres in the face of unwillingness and unresponsiveness (vv. 28, 29). Faced over and over again with unwillingness and unreadiness, the compassion of God perseveres. Finally, it is a compassion which spares, when all reason for sparing is long past (vv. 30, 31). Many a time the people of God merited the blow that would wipe them out of existence. That blow was always withheld because of the compassion of God.

The third line of revelation is the revelation of sin. Both general and particular. In general, the people of God insisted on being like the unconverted as though regenerating and saving grace had never come their way. Concerning the Egyptians we read, 'For thou knewest that they dealt proudly' (9:10). That is the mark of the unconverted, proud and arrogant. But in verse sixteen we read of the children of God, 'They and our fathers dealt proudly,' as though the grace of God had never come their way. People of God sin by insisting on behaving like the unconverted. The people of God sin by failing to behave like their God. And this is the cardinal sin of the people of God. The sin of disobedience. He keeps his word, but they will not keep his word (vv. 16, 17, 28, 29). In verses thirty-three and thirty-four, the matter is brought up to date. There is the revelation of what sin is, it is disobeying what God has said. It is turning aside from what God has required. It is revolting against his commandments.

These lines of revelation gripped the hearts of the people who first heard them. They saw a sovereign God and they longed to be right with him. They saw a compassionate God and his love moved their hearts. They saw the sin of disobedience and they longed to be rid of it. Therefore, specifically they came to God and said, 'Because of all this we make sure covenant' (v. 38). The sin of disobedience was revealed and they said, 'We will have done with it, we will dedicate ourselves to obey the law of God.' That must be a hallmark of the city of God. That must be a foundation principle of living the life of the city of God. But the word of God is not only honoured in theory and in concept but is also honoured in the practical obedience of everyday life. There is no other definition of sin than that it contravenes the will and law of God and there is no other definition of holiness except that it obeys and conforms to what God requires.

We have seen how the word of God leads the people to dedication and that dedication is the specific contrary of their sin. We come now to the remainder of the

Studies in the Book of Nehemiah

story. The way of dedication and the problem of perseverance. It is one thing to dedicate, it is another thing to keep at it.

So they come to God in the bounds of a national covenant. A deliberate policy of putting right the very thing that was wrong. But in particular they mark out certain areas of obedience for themselves. It is as if they said, 'We want to obey the whole of the law of God, but there are particular areas of obedience which are particularly relevant to us as we seek to live the life of the city of God.' Here are those particularly relevant areas of obedience.

The purity of God's people, 'That we would not give our daughters unto the people of the land nor take their daughters for our sons' (10:30). In particular, they eschewed all possibility of marriage outside the people of God, and this remains a Biblical commandment to this day. But here it is visibly in Nehemiah's city. That is the way in which a certain area of obedience was expressed, but it enshrines this principle of obedience. The people of God must live in the love of the fellowship of the people of God, and they must preserve a distinction and a separation between those who are the people of God and those who are not the people of God. Now I know that separation can be corrupted into isolation, and the proper distinctiveness of the people of God can be corrupted into an improper exclusivism. But this theme in the Bible of separation is part of the missionary theme. If the people of God are going to go to the heathen and declare the truth of God and invite acceptance of that truth, they must have a distinct way of life in which to invite the outsider. And if they lose that distinctiveness there is nothing to invite the outsider into. In the days of Ezra and Nehemiah the motivation was not an ungodly and unbiblical exclusivism and isolationism. The motivation was to preserve on the earth this distinct people whose very way of life would in itself be a distinctive testimony to the whole world. This is the truth that Jesus referred to when he spoke of his people as a city set upon a hill which cannot be hid. However, we must be careful. Separation just as a concept is of no value whatsoever. There is no point in being different just for difference sake.

In verse thirty-one they came to a second matter of specific dedication. The honouring of God's pattern for life, 'And if the people of the land bring ware or victuals on the sabbath day to sell we would not buy them on the sabbath or on a holy day and that we would let lie fallow the seventh year and the exaction of every debt.' The pattern of the one day in seven and the one year in seven. The requirements of the law of God for the life of the people of God. In particular, they were safeguarding the sabbath day. Notice the rather clever way in which they did it. They could never be accused of trying to foist their ideas upon anybody else. What they said was, 'You come here selling on the sabbath if you like, but we are not going to buy.' They honoured the day of God. And again we should search Holy Scripture to find out how to keep the day of God. Please do not allow yourself to be bound by traditional things. Go back to Scripture and discover the richness of the Lord's day. The richness of the possibility of activity and refreshments upon the day of God. The richness of the possibility of duty and involvement upon the day of God. The principle is still there of the one day in seven for the people of God. But if you want to broaden out this matter, it is that they accepted it as right and proper that God should stamp his pattern upon their lives. As far as they were concerned that was the one day in seven and the one year in seven. It is the hallmark of the citizen of the city of God that he spreads out his time before God and invites him to impose his pattern on it.

The third matter in which they felt called to a particular dedicatory obedience was in the maintenance of God's work (vv. 32–39). The ministry of the sacrifices, a charge to maintain the sacrificial services of the house of God. That is to say, a primary charge self-imposed for the maintenance of gospel ordinances. God first in relation to our possessions, 'And to bring the first fruits' (v. 35). They also charged themselves to proportionate giving to the cause of God and the tithes (v. 37). There were three high points of dedicatory obedience as they made their national covenant. Commitment to the fellowship of the people of God. And commitment to taking responsibility for God's cause.

Nehemiah went back to the King and then returned to Jerusalem. And when he returned what did he find? They had promised to give the annual contribution. They had promised to give the first fruits. They had promised to give the tithes. But now the room for storing the tithes was not needed (v. 3:4, 10). Nehemiah came back and found the promise broken. What else did he find? They had promised that if the heathen came selling they would not buy. But here they are engaged in their own commerce on the sabbath day (v. 15). They had solemnly pledged themselves to preserve the marital purity of the people of God but they did not keep that promise (v. 23). It is one thing to promise, it is another thing to keep the promise. They came to those high points of dedication. They promised to keep the law of God and preserve marriage purity. They said they would love and preserve from taint the fellowship of the people of God, and they would maintain the work of the house of God. But they did none of these things. When Nehemiah came back it would have been very easy for him to say, 'Look what you did when my back was turned. You can't get on without me, can you.' He did not, instead, 'I contended with the rulers and said why is the house of God forsaken' (v. 11). He did not point them to himself as the guardian of their conscience. He pointed them to their God and to their responsibility to God and to their forgetfulness of God.

Nehemiah continues, 'Then I contended with the nobles of Judah, and said "What evil thing is this that you do to profane the sabbath? Did not our fathers thus, and did not our God bring all this evil upon us, and upon this city? Yet you bring more wrath upon Israel."' He did not point to his own absence, and their forgetfulness of what he had done. He pointed to God and their forgetfulness of the wrath of God. It is easier and more dangerous to fall out with God, than to fall in with Satan. But if we keep in with God we will always be out with Satan. 'I contended with them,' states Nehemiah (13:25). He contended on the point of their mixed marriages. Their forgetfulness was of God. If God had dominated their thoughts they could not have forgotten his house. They could not have been careless of his wrath. They could not have slipped into sin against him, if only God had dominated their thoughts. It is lovely to end the book of Nehemiah virtually where we began. 'O God of heaven, the great and awesome God.' There is a way of perseverance my beloved, it is through allowing the word of God daily to keep the vision of God fresh before our eyes.

The B.B.C. Overseas Broadcast Address – 11th July 1976

by the Revd. Eric J. Alexander, M.A., B.D.

For just over one hundred years large numbers of people have gathered at Keswick for a whole week each July. For one reason, to meet with God and to study his word. To many listening to this broadcast that may seem a most irrelevant thing for 5,000 people to do with their time in this desperately needy world of 1976. What can a religion that is 2,000 years old have to do with the highly complex technological world of the late 20th century? The world has changed beyond all recognition since Biblical times so what can that ancient book have to say that would be relevant to our modern world. I find today that there are countless people whose problem about Christianity is precisely this. They are not intolerant or hostile, they just don't see what relevance the Christian faith has to contemporary man in this nuclear age. They are rather like the senior school-boy who wrote sometime ago to me: 'If you want me to tell you honestly what I think about Christianity I would have to put it this way; it seems to me to belong to the same world as Gothic architecture and English pageantry. An interesting curio from the past, but with nothing whatever to do with the complex modern world in which we live today.' Well, those of us who are here for the Keswick Convention believe passionately that there is nothing in the whole world so relevant for our contemporary society as the message we are here to proclaim. And in these few moments I want to try to tell you why we are so sure about that by asking you to think carefully about three things.

Although there is no question that the whole world has changed dramatically all around us (perhaps never more so than in our own generation) we are running away from the truth if we imagine that man himself has changed in the same way as his environment. The fact is that the heart of man is essentially the same as it was 200 or 2,000 years ago, and I can demonstrate that to you very simply. Why do you think, for example, that the plays of a man like Shakespeare still have such an appeal to modern men. It's not just because Shakespeare's English is so remarkable. It is because, with his profound insight into human nature, the people he is describing are not just Elizabethan men. They are modern men. So you get an unscrupulous businessman like Shylock determined to get his last pound of flesh. Or, you get a group of men jockeying for political power, careless about everything except their own future and their own ambitions as in Julius Caesar. Or, you get a depressive, lonely, isolated figure like Hamlet. They are all modern men. But come back further with me into the early chapters of the Old Testament. Here is a man consumed with jealousy of his brother. That jealousy burns into hatred, and the hatred breaks out into violence, and he strikes out and murders him.

Do we not have men like Cain in our modern world?

B.B.C. Broadcast Address

Here is a man whose only interest in life is his appetite. And to satisfy his desire for material things he will sell his soul. Have we advanced beyond men like Esau in our modern society? Here is a man called David who has power and possession and in an idle moment he catches sight of another man's wife, and decides that he must have her. It doesn't matter to him whether he's smashing up a family or ruining her husband, he only cares about himself. Do we not have men like that in our modern world? But someone may be saying, surely you're not going to compare modern man flying in his sophisticated super-sonic jet with ancient man in his home-made chariot travelling at fourteen miles an hour. Well think about it! What is the real difference between them? It's merely the speed at which they are travelling; the object of their journey is exactly the same. They're either going to do business or seek pleasure, to make love or to make war. The great testimony of the Bible and history is that the heart of man is exactly the same as it always has been. And that's a fact from which we dare not run away.

The second thing is this. The source of all the world's problems doesn't lie in man's changing environment, but in man himself. It's in his selfishness, his greed, his misuse of so many of God's good gifts. Isn't that what we are being driven to see today, however reluctantly? With all our new skills and astonishing scientific advance, for which Christians thank God, we find we can control so much. We can control a man's journey to the moon and land him there safely, but we can't control his behaviour here on earth. So it's possible for us to have men on the moon and hell on earth, despite the conferences of politicians and the efforts of statesmen. It's precisely because of the unsolved problem of man himself that the world trembles because man's discoveries are likely to be the means of his destruction. Jesus put the problem very forcefully and clearly in Mark chapter seven. It is not, he said, the things from 'without' that spoil a man but the things from 'within'. Out of a man's heart come evil thoughts, fornication, theft, murder, adultery, ruthless greed and malice, fraud, indecency, envy, slander, arrogance, folly. The heart of the human problem is the problem of the human heart. And that's true about nations, families or personal relationships and wherever you live.

Here's the third and last thing that I want you to think about with me. The unique and glorious thing about the authentic Christian Gospel is that while it is concerned with the needs of a changing society and a changing world it doesn't stop there. It goes right down to the intractable problem of the human heart where man is out of control. The promise of God in the Bible is: A new heart will I give you, and a new spirit will I put within you. The apostles proclaimed that if any man is in Christ he is a new creature, old things are passed away, everything has become new. That is neither hearsay, nor ancient history. We as Christians bear witness to the fact that Jesus Christ has touched our lives with his love and power. We believe that the Christian Gospel is not just relevant, but that it is the only relevant word for this modern world with all its agonising problems. What could be more relevant than a Saviour who touches that deepest area of the world's need and brings hope to a society which groans in every part of the earth?

New Testament Christianity is not just about a new social order and a new standard of living. It is about that and infinitely more. It is about our radical, spiritual and moral change which the Bible calls a new birth. The unique message of the Christian faith is that Jesus comes not just to show us a better way of life, but to give us wise counsel. He comes to enter into those broken needy lives of ours and by his power lift burdens, cleanse consciences, break habits, change characters and live out his risen life through us. In the New Testament this is what being a Christian is all about. It is Christ living in me.

Before I conclude, let me bring all that down to a personal level. If indeed as Jesus says the heart of the human problem is the problem of the human heart, then that's where your greatest need lies wherever you are in the world today. How eagerly we run away from that truth. Oh, we say, 'If my circumstances were just different, if I lived in a difference place, or if the people around me would just change, or if I had another job,' we often say. Now all these things can be problems, but they are not the ultimate problem. Jesus, who is a master at diagnosis, puts his finger on the deepest problem of all. From within, he says. Out of the heart comes every evil thing. I want to say to you that if you are without Christ, if you have no indwelling Saviour living in you, then no revolution in your circumstances will meet your ultimate need. It is only Christ the Revolutionary from within that can do that. By his death on the Cross as our sin-bearer he offers us pardon for our past. By his resurrection he brings us power for the present. And by the promise of his return in glory he brings us hope for the future.

CHRISTIANS UNDER PRESSURE
(Romans 5:1-5)

by the Revd. Gordon Bridger, M.A.

I read recently of a room in a Whitehall basement in London where Winston Churchill used to meet with his war cabinet. In that room there was a notice, apparently attributed to Queen Victoria – 'Please understand that there is no depression in this house. We are not interested in the possibilities of defeat, they do not exist.' A splendid thought, but how realistic?

Christians suffer in various ways from many types of pressure. There are the pressures from within – men like Jacob, Peter and Solomon faced these inward pressures caused by the sin that dwells within us. And certainly Paul knew of these inward tensions and pressures, as he writes to the Christians in Galatia, 'The Spirit lusteth against flesh and the flesh against the Spirit.' And most of us can identify readily with that kind of conflict. Yet it is a fact that even under these tensions and battles within that are part of the Christian experience, Paul can write on a note of victory. 'Who would deliver me from the body of this death?' he asks. And immediately replies triumphantly, 'I thank my God through Jesus Christ our Lord.'

Christians under Pressure

But as well as tensions within, there are pressures that come from outside. And they are what Paul is concerned with in this particular passage. 'Since we are justified by faith we have peace with God through our Lord Jesus Christ,' he says, 'More than that, we rejoice in our sufferings.' And the word 'sufferings' or 'tribulations' used here is a Greek word really meaning 'pressures'. Paul knew what pressure was – the pressure of persecution, opposition, unpopularity, probably of illness and overwork. And yet the apostle could say with confidence in the Lord, 'We rejoice even in the midst of these pressures.'

The question I want to consider is this: How can we as Christians have victory both when the inner conflicts and the outward pressures of life seem so great? The physical and mental pressures that we have to face, such as illness, overtiredness or overwork. The pressure of living in an increasingly secular society. There are the pressures of middle age, perhaps the fear of failure, or of redundancy. 'Will I be wanted any more?' 'Where shall I live?' 'How can I make ends meet?' I hardly need enumerate them, because I am sure we are all aware of the types of pressures we have to face today, just as Paul did in his day. The important question to which we must find an answer is: 'What is the secret of overcoming, of finding victory in the midst of these pressures?'

I want to suggest that in these verses, Paul unfolds four. The first I would call *my relationship to Jesus*. This is fundamental to all that Paul is going to say. It is described here as being justified by faith in union with Jesus – this is what our relationship means. Here are three things about this relationship. Firstly, it signifies that we are as vitally united to Jesus as a branch is to the vine, that we have his life flowing through us in our lives. Paul uses the metaphor of grafting to show how the two are fused together (this is the meaning of the Greek word translated as 'united' in Romans 6:5). Secondly, this relationship is characterised by a complete exchange. Paul says, 'Therefore, since we are justified by faith, we have peace with God.' This word 'therefore' refers back to his argument in chapter four, where he describes what justification by faith in Jesus means. Quoting from the Psalms, he uses in verse eight the word 'reckon'. Now this is an accounting term. Paul is saying that when I am justified by faith in Jesus, joined to him by faith in him, a great exchange takes place. My sins that have separated me from God are removed from my account and laid to the account of Jesus – they are 'reckoned' to him, and on the cross he bore them in my place. But that is not all. Paul is saying that Jesus' righteousness is put to my account. So, not only is my debt of sin removed from me and laid on Jesus, but moreover the riches of God's grace, through the righteousness of Jesus are laid to my account. I am dead to sin, no longer under sin's judgement, and I have peace with God. May we illustrate this simply. It would be a marvellous thing if, when I was in great debt and knew I was doomed to prison, a friend came along and said, 'Look, I'm rich, I'll pay the debt off for you.' That would be tremendous. But how much more tremendous it would be if my friend said to me, 'Not only will I pay the debt, I will put into your bank account all my riches, and you will never need to be in debt again. Whenever you like, you can go to your bank and find available there the riches that I have put to your account.' This is the situation that Paul is describing in Romans chapters four and five. And so, because I am united to Jesus by faith in him, whatever the pressures within, whatever

Christians under Pressure

the pressures from outside, I can have peace with God, for not only are my sins no longer laid to my account, but I also have access to the 'grace in which I stand'. Through Jesus I have the wisdom, the power and the strength that I need to endure to the end.

Then there is one other thing I want to say about this relationship with Jesus. It is characterised by a vital union, by a complete exchange, and thirdly by a certain hope. Paul writes: 'Therefore, since we are justified by faith, we have peace with God through our Lord Jesus Christ. Through him we have obtained access to this grace in which we stand, and we rejoice in our hope of sharing the glory of God.' The Christian hope is a certain and expectant hope, and Paul's triumphant, confident attitude in the midst of pressures from both within and outside is a result of his knowledge that he is justified by faith in Jesus. And if justified, he will be glorified, for if God has begun this work in him, he will most certainly complete it. 'For those he foreknew he also predestined to be conformed to the image of his Son . . . And those whom he predestined he also called; and those whom he called, he also justified; and those whom he justified he also glorified.' (Romans 8:29, 30). Therefore the sufferings of this life are not to be compared with the glory that is to come – because of our union with Jesus, justified by faith, with a certain hope of glory, we can rejoice in our sufferings.

Paul goes on, there is a second truth we must understand if we are to be victorious under pressure. He writes 'And we rejoice in our hope of sharing the glory of God. More than that, we rejoice in our sufferings.' This is the fundamental importance of our attitude to suffering and to pressure. The fact that I am justified in Christ does not mean that I automatically rejoice in tribulation. Even as a Christian I may still resent my circumstances, just as the Israelites in the wilderness despite all the privileges of God's care shown to them did not rejoice and were often resentful of their circumstances. I believe that not only is it possible to rejoice in our sufferings, but we are commanded to do so.

It should help us to remember that Christians should expect suffering. Jesus said, 'The servant is not greater than his master; if they hate me they will hate you.' And in the letter to the Hebrews it is made clear that suffering is a discipline, and thus becomes the very mark of sonship. But I think there are two points we need to bear in mind on the subject of rejoicing in suffering. Firstly, rejoicing means to boast, to glory in, to exult – but not necessarily to enjoy. We do not enjoy our sufferings, but we can nevertheless rejoice under pressure. In one of his letters, Paul says that we are as sorrowful, yet always rejoicing, as if the two things are not always incompatible. A Christian may sometimes feel sorrowful under the pressures he suffers, and yet not be resentful, not grumble against God, but be glad in him. Secondly, rejoicing in our Lord in the midst of suffering is not quite the same thing as rejoicing in suffering, or, to use a popular modern phrase, 'Thanking God for everything.' I don't think God has called us to thank him for suffering, but we can thank him *in* suffering – 'In everything give thanks.' We can even thank God on account of suffering, because we see as Paul goes on to say, that suffering can do great things for us under God. Even in a difficult, painful situation, Christians have the grace and freedom to look for something for which they can honestly and without hypocrisy thank God.

Christians, then, rejoice in suffering and should ex-

Christians under Pressure

pect the good fruit of tribulation. First because of our *relationship to Jesus*, secondly because of our *attitude of rejoicing*, and thirdly because of our *understanding of providence*. Notice what Paul says in these verses 'More than that, we rejoice in our sufferings *knowing that* suffering (pressures, tribulation) produces endurance, and endurance produces character, and character produces hope, and hope does not disappoint us, because God's love has been poured into our hearts through the Holy Spirit which has been given to us.' He can rejoice because he knows something – this 'something' is the providence of God. The Bible teaches that God's providence is sometimes preventive (he sometimes prevents evil coming to his children, as when he put a hedge around Job for a time), but also permissive (he permits evil actions of men, and of course Christians suffer as much as others), but he only permits suffering because God's providence is also purposive. 'We know,' says Paul in his letter to the Romans, 'that God works all things together for good to those who love him and who are called according to his purpose' *(8:28)*. In chapter five he says that we know suffering works for our good because God is in control. It produces endurance, character and hope. This word 'character' means that we have been tested and proved genuine. As Peter puts it in his first letter, 'In this you rejoice, though now for a little while you may have to suffer various trials, so that the genuineness of your faith, more precious than gold which though perishable is tested with fire, may rebound to praise and glory and honour at the revelation of Jesus Christ' (1:6). The world today desperately needs to see that our faith is genuine, so if you are under pressure and you're enduring, believing and rejoicing in spite of it all, and indeed on account of it, the world can see that your faith is the real thing, and God is thus glorified.

Tribulation also allows us to share his holiness, for it yields the peaceable fruit of righteousness. If therefore we are looking at our problems and pressure in the light of God's purpose for us, we not only rejoice, because they produce endurance and character, but also because they lead us to the certain hope that we will share his glory.

The last secret of rejoicing in tribulation is the *experience of the Spirit*. 'This hope does not disappoint us because God's love has been poured into our hearts through the Holy Spirit which has been given to us.' John Stott makes here the distinction between two Greek verbs. When we read 'The Holy Spirit was given,' the reference is to a past event, when we first became Christians. When we read of God's love being poured into us, it is a perfect tense referring to a past event with abiding results. In other words, the Spirit goes on pouring his love into our hearts if we will open our hearts to him. In this way, through the experience of God's love being poured into our hearts by the Holy Spirit, we are enabled to bring forth the good fruit of endurance, and character, and hope even in the midst of pressures.

In this dry summer, I have learnt two things about gardening. One is that if you want to harvest really good potatoes, you must let them die back first. When I saw this happening I thought the sun had shrivelled them and they were no good, but I was told that this is an essential stage in their growth. The other thing is that potatoes need constant watering. These two facts seem to me to sum up what Paul is saying in our passage. If the Spirit of God is to fill my heart with his love so

Christians under Pressure

that I know without any shadow of doubt that whatever pressures and conflicts I'm facing I can have the victory in Christ and rejoice in him, then first I need to die to self. There is no room for the love of God in me if I am full of love for myself. But more than that, as I open my life to his Spirit, he goes on pouring the refreshing water of his love into my heart. So, in order to win the victory even when under the many pressures that Christians face today, we may reckon on our relationship with Jesus, which allows us to rejoice in suffering and tribulation, and we may rest on the knowledge of God's providence working on our behalf in love, and respond to the daily pouring forth of his love and power through the Holy Spirit into my life.

'I SAW THE LORD'
(Isa. 6:1-7)

by the Revd. Michael Cole, M.A.

In Isaiah chapter six there are three truths for examination; the contrasts that Isaiah saw. The first was a contrast between people. In verse one we read that 'The year in which King Uzziah died I saw the Lord.' The contrast there is between the earthly throne that was empty, and the heavenly throne that was holy. It was not the fact that the king had died that impressed the people, it was the reason why the king had died.

The story is given to us in full detail in second Chronicles chapter twenty-six, where we have the account of Uzziah coming to the throne when sixteen years old and reigning for fifty-two years. The writer informs us that he set himself to seek the Lord. What a marvellous aim for a young person, sixteen years old setting himself to seek the Lord. How different that may be from the aim of some of us who at sixteen are setting just to fulfil ourselves.

Uzziah began as a good and God-fearing king. He was a man of power and that led on to him being a king of prosperity. His success and the increase in his wealth, we are told on two occasions, were because God made him to prosper. God helped him because he sought the way of the Lord. His fame spread far because he was marvellousy helped but then his pride set in. He tried to take on the duty of a priest, to offer a sacrifice, and the priest rebuked him. The king in turn rebuked the priest, and God judged the king and leprosy broke out on his face and body. The king, who had been the admiration of the whole nation, died an outcast and a leper.

Here is a contrast in persons. The first person, the earthly king whose throne is now empty. And the other person, God himself sitting upon a throne high and lifted up; and his train filled the temple (v. 1). The earthly throne was to be reoccupied again but the psalmist tells us that God's throne endures for ever and ever. At this point we should ask ourselves this question: where do I look for my standard of living? Because here is a contrast between an earthly leader and God himself. If we compare ourselves with other people we may think we are not doing badly, but if we compare ourselves with the eternal God we begin to see ourselves as God sees us.

The second contrast was in worship. Isaiah presents a picture of heavenly worship. The seraphim, a marvellous visual aid for worship, bright and glorious. But they covered their faces and feet so that God was the only person seen to be worshipped. They took great care in the worship of God, it was to be pure and perfect, holy and right. But what a contrast with the worship of the day. The worship that the people were prepared to offer was second best, was ill prepared. What a contrast between human worship and heavenly worship. 'What to me is the multitude of your sacrifices?' says the Lord, 'I have had enough of burnt offerings of rams and the fat of fed beasts: I do not delight in the blood of bulls, or of lambs, or of he goats.' The worship that was being offered to God was not acceptable to a holy God. Among evangelicals there has been a new move to make our worship acceptable to God, but on our standards of worship which has been set by another earthly pattern, rather than by the pure and sinless pattern of heaven. Do we, like the prophet, need to be reminded of this contrast between human worship and the heavenly worship that the holy God deserves and desires?

The third contrast is between the faithlessness of the people and the faithfulness of God. And here we need to ask some questions. How are you husband in your faithfulness as a husband? How are you in your faithfulness as a wife? How faithful are we as Christian workers, in Christian witness, prayer, giving? How are we in our faithfulness in matters of sex, honesty, speech? That is not my list because if you look at some of the New Testament epistles you will find that those were the very questions that were addressed to Christians in the early Church. It was in those areas of life that their practical faithfulness was to be seen.

Isaiah then made a confession, 'I am a man of unclean lips' (v. 5). It is only when we begin to see God as he truly is that we begin to see ourselves as we truly are. It was when Job saw God in his power that he abhorred himself and repented in dust and ashes. It was when Peter saw Christ's power in that miraculous catch of fish that he said 'Depart from me for I am a sinful man O Lord.' It was when John saw the vision of the glorified Christ in the book of the Revelation that he fell at his feet as dead. And it was when Isaiah saw the

'I saw the Lord'

vision of the Lord that then he said, 'Woe is me, I am lost.' However, our natural reaction is sometimes to condone it, or blame somebody else. But confession of our sin is not only spiritually good, it is not only psychologically good, it is physically good. The psalmist says that 'When I declared not my sin my body wasted away through my groaning all day long' (Psalm 32). But things began to change when he acknowledged his sin.

Notice three things about Isaiah's confession. First he confessed his sinful nature, 'I am lost.' G. K. Chesterton was once asked the question, 'What is wrong with the world?' His simple answer was, 'I am.' He then went on to confess specifically. He said, 'I am a man of unclean lips.' He specified what was wrong, and maybe we need to be much more specific in our confession of sin, so that we may be assured that God has forgiven that particular sin. When David confessed his sin, Nathan came and said that the Lord had taken away his sin. It was a specific confession, and it was a definite forgiveness. Then there is a third thing about his confession. His sin was related to his strong point. We often feel that sin is linked with our weaknesses, but here is Isaiah confessing a sin that is related to his service. His lips were to be used, they were his strongest asset. But he confesses that even that which is strong and given over to the Lord's service was marked by sin. There is danger in being proud of the strong point in our Christian life and service.

The third marvellous truth is the cleansing that Isaiah experienced. What a marvellous picture of God's provision here. Isaiah writes that the seraphim touched his mouth with a burning coal and said, 'This has touched your lips, your guilt is taken away, your sin is forgiven' (v. 7) God took something from the temple and applied it to the prophet himself. And we can turn our hearts to the Lord Jesus and it is as if God takes the saving cleansing blood of the Lord Jesus and says, this has touched that part of your life that is marred by sin. Sin not only is an offence to us and makes us ashamed and guilty. Sin is an offence to God. But Isaiah was not only told his guilt was taken away, he was also told that his sin was forgiven. And that is the cleansing that you and I can experience through the blood of the Lord Jesus that goes on cleansing us from all sin.

'AND THE LORD BLESSED HIM THERE' (Genesis 32:39)

by the Revd. George B. Duncan, M.A.

I want us to find the secret of what happened at Peniel. The name Peniel means the face of God and that really is the secret of what happened there. To help us find the secret of what happened there I will ask three simple questions.

The first question is: *'Where did the Lord bless this man?'* In trying to answer that question I am not so much concerned about the physical location as the spiritual condition in which we find the man. But the physical location and the spiritual condition are both very closely linked. The first thing we discover is that God blessed Jacob in a place where he was alone (v. 24). We need to get hold of this fact that any valid experience of the grace and goodness of God is something essentially between a man and his God, and God had to get Jacob alone before he could do much for or with him. When God blessed him it was when he was alone. The family, the flocks, the herds, the servants had all gone, and their noise had gone with them. Maybe Jacob could only see the distant glow of a fire and hear the bark of a wakeful dog or the bleat of a sheep. But essentially he was utterly alone and above him was spread the dome of the heavens lit only with the soft and silent light of the stars. We need not only to be alone but quiet. But not only was the Lord able to bless this man when he was in a place where he was alone, but when he was in a state when he was afraid *(v. 7)*. He was afraid of Esau, that was the superficial and obvious fear. But in the opening verse of this incident we sense another and deeper fear. He was afraid of this man who had intruded, and who was wrestling with him. I think early on Jacob realised that this was not a man with a small 'm' but a man with a capital 'M'. He was wrestling, and God was wrestling with him and he was afraid. Surely that was why the struggle went on so long. It went on from dusk until dawn and if he hadn't been afraid of his Lord the wrestling would have ceased as soon as he knew. I wonder if that describes the spiritual condition in which some of us are found? Orthodox evangelical Christians, but deep, deep down afraid of God. Afraid of what God will say to us. Afraid of what God will ask of us. Are you afraid of what God will do with you? Like Jacob we have our other fears, the pressures and problems that we can't cope with, but is there deeper still this deeper fear? But that was where God blessed this man, in a place where he was alone and in a state in which he was afraid.

'When did God bless this man?' This second question is simple enough for each of us to get the grip and the thrust of what I believe God wants us to consider underlying this text, 'And he blessed him there.' In this second question I am asking not simply *where* but *when* did God bless this man? The answer again seems to lie in the text of the Scripture. I believe that God blessed

'And The Lord Blessed Him There'

Jacob first of all when an intensity came into his praying. A man said, 'Let me go for the day breaketh.' And Jacob said, 'I will not let thee go except thou bless me.' When an intensity came into his praying Jacob came to the point where he cried out, 'I will not let thee go except thou bless me.' 'Ask and we shall receive,' said Jesus Christ, and when the Lord gave a picture of what praying can be like, he talked of a man hammering on the door of a neighbour at midnight. Years ago I came across a phrase I have never forgotten, 'What is the intensity of your desire?' What is the intensity of our praying? How much time do we give to it? How much genuine desire do our prayers contain? What do we want? How badly do we want it? When Paul spoke of prayer he likened it to the travail of childbirth.

But not only did an intensity come into his praying, an integrity came into his thinking. This was a bit tougher. We read of the Lord saying to Jacob, *'What is your name?'* And he said 'Jacob.' The question was a challenge to be honest about himself. Outwardly Jacob had done very well, but spiritually he was a bankrupt. Self-interest had determined his every action. He had deceived his blind father, he had never bothered about the vows he had made at Bethel, he had outwitted the cunning of Laban and the only redeeming fact was his love for Rachel. Jacob was what we would call a rotter. He was a cheat, he wasn't honest with anybody. He was a deceiver and before the Lord could bless him an integrity had to come into his thinking about himself. He had to face the truth about himself. *What is your name?* In those days the name meant the nature, the character. 'What kind of a person are you?' God asked him. I wonder if the time when God will bless us will be the time when we are honest about ourselves. What kind of a person are you as a Christian? O I know you say you are saved. Maybe you have a right to say that, a Biblical right to say it. But what are you saved from? Are you saying, I am saved from hell. Well thank God for that, Christ came to do that, but he did more than that in his coming. He came to save us from our sins. What about your sins and mine? Bad temper, irritability, pride, self-will, selfishness, laziness, greed, unreliability, worry. Are you being saved? What kind of a Christian are you? Are you the kind of Christian that brings glory and honour to the name of Jesus Christ? Are you the kind of Christian that God can trust and use? What's your name? When did God bless this man? When an integrity came into his thinking about himself. Jesus said it was the pure in heart that would see God. He warned the pharisees that even the prostitutes would get into the kingdom of heaven before them. The pure in heart see God, the people who have nothing to hide and are utterly open and totally sincere and completely honest. They are the ones that get through to God. The tragedy about so many of us, is that we go on for so long. Jacob went on a long time, quite happy about himself, he is the only one that was. Nobody else was. Are you happy about yourself? And nobody else happy. When did God bless this man? When an *intensity* came into his praying, when an *integrity* came into his thinking.

My third and last question. *'How did God bless Jacob?'* There is nothing very difficult about these questions, but they are crucial. We can gather how the Lord blessed him if we listen first of all to what he said to him. 'Thy name shall be called no more Jacob.' In other words God said to Jacob, 'Look here Jacob there is something in your life that has been there for a long

'And The Lord Blessed Him There'

time and it has got to stop.' What was it? How did God bless this man? God's blessing is initially a call to holiness of life. It is not a lowering of the standard, it is the raising of it high. The way the Lord blesses is by raising the standard high and by calling us to holiness. Do you remember how Jesus himself spoke in a similar way to a woman dragged before him? The one taken in adultery. When he got rid of her accusers he asked the question, 'Has no man condemned thee?' Then he gave the final word of grace, 'Neither do I condemn thee.' But that wasn't all. He then said, 'Go and sin no more.' That is the blessing, the summons and the call to holiness. Consider the fairness of Jesus. 1. He did not deny the charge but he did not limit it. 2. The kindness of Jesus. He did not deal with the woman when the men were there, he waited till they had gone and dealt with her alone. He loves to deal with people alone. 3. The forgiveness of Jesus. Neither do I condemn thee... And that is the blessing. Amy Wilson Carmichael said, 'Hold them to the highest, God always does.' And that is the way he blesses. Because when we are held to the highest then our pride is shattered, so God said to Jacob, 'Jacob no more.'

But the blessing went beyond that when you examine not simply what he said *to* him, but what he said *of* him. If he held the standard high, he raised the sinner high. Raised him to the status of a prince. 'As a prince hast thou power with God and with men.' One of the commentators has suggested, and this seems to be implied in the words, 'Because thou hast had power with God, thou shalt have power with men.' The real blessing that God gives is not something he gives *to* us, but something he wants to give *through* us to others. That is the blessing of usefulness and of great joy and happiness in being useful. I think one of the sad things, one of the impossible things to bear, when people who are not Christians get old is that they become useless, and they just become a burden. A Christian is never useless. But a person who is not a Christian does become useless. People are praying that they may be taken and the burden may be removed. But the greatest blessing that God can ever give to my life is not just to give me something that is going to give me a thrill. God is going to give something to me so that he can give, through me, to others. The whole blessing that came to Jacob that day that God lifted him to a condition where he would be useable. Where he fitted into the eternal purpose of God that was going to reach to the ends of the earth.

The blessing of God will do just that for you and for me. When he speaks to us it may well be of his holiness and the requirements of it. But when he speaks of us it will be in terms of our usefulness in his hands and in his will. The two go hand in hand. Robert Murray McCheyne said, 'Study holiness of life. Your sermons last for an hour, but your life will be preaching all the week through.' So having been blessed by God at Peniel, that place which means the face of God, we read that the sun rose upon him. For sheer poetry and beauty and truth I do not know any lovelier sentence in the Old Testament than 'The sun rose upon him.' And Jacob walked away from Peniel in the radiance of the dawn.

THREE TESTS
(Luke 10)

by the Revd. George B. Duncan, M.A.

In Luke chapter ten, we find three men who called Jesus 'Lord', and each of whom found they had then to face up to certain implications. The introduction is found at the end of the previous chapter (vv. 57 to 62). A certain man, followed by two others, said 'Lord', and they found that they were faced with something that the Lord had to say to them in return. In these threefold incidents, we have what we might call three tests concerning the Lordship of Christ and our Christian discipleship.

Most of us are familiar with the idea of tests. It may be that we have had to pass an aptitude test before being accepted for a certain professional job. My two sons are both airline pilots, one with British Caledonian and the other with British Airways, and they had to pass very stringent tests before they became pilots, and you will be relieved to know that the pass mark is extremely high. They have to pass tests regularly to see if they are still fit to fly. Passing tests. It's a familiar part of life in almost every department, but I want to look at these three tests.

Keswick Seventysix

The first one may strike a slightly unexpected note. It may be that in our Lord's dealings with these individuals he was putting his finger on a special area of weakness he wanted to test them on. 'A certain man said unto him, Lord, I will follow thee whithersoever thou goest. And Jesus said to him, foxes have holes, and birds of the air have nests; but the Son of man hath not where to lay his head.' The first test is the test of *poverty*. I suggest that there is a test in Christian discipleship of our willingness to accept deprivation. A willingness and a readiness to go without. I am not, of course, suggesting that our Lord was thinking in terms of what some might call a vow of poverty such as exists in some monastic orders. Nor am I suggesting that our Lord is indicating that there is anything wrong in the possession of wealth, although if it is acquired wrongfully or used wrongfully, then our Lord would certainly condemn that. He has pointed out that wealth creates its own difficulties, but it need not. Nowhere do I find the possession of wealth condemned and our Lord isn't thinking of that. Indeed, our Lord was beholden again and again to those who appeared to have more than most people of this world's goods. The tomb in which his body was laid was that of a rich man. I am thinking, however, of how the will of God in a person's life may mean him being willing to accept a lower standard of living on a material level. The kind of example that obviously comes to mind is that of a young doctor who is so competent that he could have risen to great heights in the medical profession here at home, but has to be prepared to accept the kind of salary a doctor may be paid working for a missionary society in a distant land. The kind of situation when promotion calls for compromise in some area of principle, and therefore has to

Three Tests

be forfeited. I well remember how James Fox the rising film star came to Glasgow not long after his conversion and for the first few months of his Christian life had fellowship with us in St. George's Tron. He was under contract to perform in Glasgow in a series of plays. However, it was not long before he had to tell the director that there were some of them in which he could not act. And it was not a great surprise, although a tremendous blow, that he was told his services would be no longer required. He found that the work of Christ adds to the many demands made upon the purse of the Christian which means that we have less to spend on ourselves. I was tremendously shaken and almost shattered when I spoke recently at the Japan Keswick Convention at Hokoni. The Convention there lasted for three days, and the giving of the Japanese Christians towards the expenses of the convention averaged £10 per head. Two years ago at Keswick the average was less than £2 for a whole week. At the Lausanne Congress two years ago, one of the clauses in the covenant read 'Those of us who live in affluent circumstances accept our duty to the veil of a simpler life-style in order to contribute more generously to both relief and evangelism.' An acceptance of deprivation, the discipline that goes without. Legitimate things that maybe our neighbours can afford.

But if there is an acceptance of deprivation we find in this area an assurance of compensation. You remember when Simon Peter spoke of the cost of discipleship that he and the others had borne in terms of personal relationships and material resources. Our Lord replied 'Everyone that hath left house, or parents or brethren or wife and children for the kingdom of God's sake shall receive manifold more in this present time and in the world to come, life everlasting.' Manifold more. I wonder what he meant. Did he mean that we actually get more houses, more parents, more brethren, more wives, more children (presumably not the wives anyway!). I wonder if he meant that many people look to material possessions as the means of happiness and satisfaction. And that while people who relied on these things for happiness and contentment might find a measure of both in them, those whose obedience to his will might involve them in some degree of loss, would never be losers in terms of such happiness and contentment. They would never lose anything at all, rather they would find other riches, truer riches, they would find better happiness, deeper contentment. Nobody will ever be the poorer for following Jesus wholeheartedly. But maybe that was the weak area in this man who called Jesus 'Lord'.

The second test was, 'Follow me.' To which the second man replied, 'Lord, suffer me first to go and bury my father.' But Jesus said to him, 'Let the dead bury their own dead, but go thou and preach the kingdom of God.' I call this the test of *urgency*. How casual the matter of discipleship seemed to this man. He didn't mean it literally. His reply in effect was 'all right, I will, but not just now; when it suits me. I don't know exactly when that will be, just as I don't know when my father will die.' The whole thing being treated casually. The call for men was sounded by Gideon when the Spirit of the Lord had come upon him and many thousands treated the whole business casually. They took their time to drink and rested. Only three hundred pressed on urgently, eagerly, anxiously wanting to come to grips with the enemy, and while the nine thousand seven hundred lounged and lazed at the brook, three hundred

Three Tests

leapt across it and pressed on up the hill. The test of urgency is a test that most disciples of the Lord today fail. How casually the vast majority of so-called Christians are treating the will and the work of the King. It's decided by the weather, our convenience or a television programme. Is there any urgency about our Christian living today? How often it is that the vast majority of Christians are little more than spectators. I wonder if the reason is simply that they haven't passed the test of urgency. Do you treat your loyalty to Jesus Christ as a nice hobby? If it's not too demanding and if it's not too much of a bother, then maybe you will turn up, and just show willing. Is there anything casual about the advance of communism today? There's an urgency. It's carefully planned, ruthlessly executed. It demands total obedience and total commitment and the Church thinks it's going to laze its way to victory. But it will not happen that way. Years ago in a young people's meeting I heard the Revd. Laurie Sheath say that the worst sin in the Christian life is laziness. The test of urgency. Do we pass that test in the Lordship of Christ?

My road ends with the test of *sovereignty*. Another person also said, 'Lord, I will follow thee, but . . . ' Here was an involvement that proved unacceptable. We have a man offering to Christ an obedience that was partial. It was the kind of obedience that was all Abraham was willing to offer initially, and which nearly brought him and God's plan for him to disaster. In Genesis chapter twelve, we read that God told him 'Get thee out of thy country from thy kindred from thy father's house, into a land that I will show thee.' And he did most of that, but not all. We read repeatedly 'Lot went with him.' *(12:15; 13:1, 5.)* He obeyed as far as it suited him. But when it didn't suit him, he didn't obey. His obedience was partial and I wouldn't be a bit surprised if it was true of every single Christian who hears and reads these words. There is something in our lives that we are not prepared to hand over to his control. An involvement that proved unacceptable, an enthronement that proves inescapable. 'Whosoever will come after me, let him deny himself,' say 'no' to himself. Saying 'no' to ourselves means saying 'yes' to Christ. The will of God is designed to cover every area of my life, my character, my conduct, my career. No restriction, no limitation anywhere is permitted. One of the loveliest prayers is that of Epaphras where Paul tells the Colossian Christians that he is praying that they may 'Stand perfect and complete in all the will of God.' He says: 'Understanding the will of God is our problem. Undertaking the will of God is our privilege. Undercutting the will of God is our peril.' This man called him Lord, but . . .

As far as you are concerned, is he Lord? He ought to be. He must be. Are you prepared to tell him that he is? Tell him now and tell him again and again he is not only Saviour, he is Lord. The test of *poverty,* the test of *urgency*, the test of *sovereignty*, all passed. Jesus is Lord.

A LEADER IN LOVE

by the Revd. Tom Houston

Some big churches, some small, some growing, others declining, some alive, some dead, some have great ministers, some have terrible ministers, some have warm fellowship and others are very cold. There is nothing new about this. The churches to which Paul wrote in the New Testament were a very mixed bag, and when John was given the visions at the beginning of the book of Revelation, it was in the first instance to seven very different churches in Asia. Some are hotly orthodox like Ephesus, others are gullible and compromising like the church in Pergamon. Some are doing better than at the beginning like Thyatira. Others, on the other hand, have lost their first love like Ephesus. Some have trouble with their budget like Smyrna. Others are very rich like Laodicea. Laying them side by side they all have some good features and they all have some flaws. Jesus sees both. And it will help us to do the same if we look at the point at which John starts in the Revelation. He breaks into praise in the beginning of the chapter, and then in this doxology he says it all. 'To him who loves us and has freed us from our sins by his blood and made us a kingdom, priests to his God and Father, to him be glory and dominion for ever and ever' (Revelation 1:5, 6).

The first thing, 'He loves us.' This is where it begins and never ends. The old theologians used to make a distinction between what they called the love of complacency and the love of benevolence. There are some things and some people you like or you love because they please you. That's the love of complacency. But there's very much in us that does not please God and so he cannot always love us with the love of complacency. That's where the other comes in. God wants good things to happen to us. He wants us to become good and that's the love of benevolence, and it continues even in the face of what displeases him.

The Ephesians had left their first love, but Jesus cannot even use the idea of a first love, or a later love, or lack of it because he loves the Ephesians equally all the time. The people in Smyrna may be slandered by others but Jesus loved them. He sees what is true and assures them of his constancy in sustaining them while they are about to suffer even more things than in the past. The people in that church in Pergamon were not all that sound and they had a group of people who had some very weird ideas and very questionable practices, but the love of Jesus for them was sure, leading him to send them this word. The people in Thyatira might have some who had come under the spell of a dominant woman with a phony gift of prophecy. Nonetheless, the living Lord continued to love them. Sardus had all the reputation of being a live church yet in reality it was dying on its feet. Still Jesus kept loving them. Philadelphia might only have a little strength, so the message says, but they were loved a lot. Laodicea might make Jesus sick with their complacency in blowing hot and cold but he went on loving them, indeed this is one place where he says it again, 'Whom I love, I reprove.'

This is the most healing truth in the whole world. Edward Irving was an outstanding and yet tragic figure in the last century. Once he walked into a house, in his pontifical way, where a little boy lay dying. He strode straight through to the bedroom, looked at the boy lying in the bed, put his hand on his head and said, 'My boy, God loves you.' And he walked out. He didn't say another word to anybody in the house. A little later the boy came running through from his bedroom saying to his mother, 'God loves me, God loves me, God loves me.' The boy didn't die. He lived. The sense of being loved healed. God is love and Jesus is the one who showed us what that meant in human terms.

Secondly, 'He liberated us.' He has freed us from our sins. Here the tense changes. This is a past event. He says when it was. Jesus set us free when he died on the cross. The completeness of what Jesus did on the cross was important to John. It is he who reports Jesus as saying in that last prayer, 'I have finished the work that you gave me to do.' And all through the Revelation the title of honour given to Jesus is 'The lamb who was slain so that he might ransom men for God by his blood.' It's the same picture. Slaves are ransomed at great cost. It leads to their liberty, but liberty from what? As I wrote out this Scripture in as many versions as I could find, I discovered that all the words changed at one part of the sentence or the other, but there was one phrase that didn't change. It was, 'From our sins.' There is no other way to say that. What we need to be liberated from are our sins. Jesus did this on the cross.

Keswick Seventysix

The Apostle John had reason to know. Jesus set John free from bigoted party spirit (Mark 9). John had an ambitious mother who pushed her two boys into ambitious ways. But Jesus liberated him from unhealthy ambition. John had a vindictive streak in him wanting to call down fire from heaven on the Samaritain villagers. From all these sinful tendencies, from all these sins, Jesus liberated John by his blood and made him into the revered old Apostle of Love. The freedom that John thanked him for was very real to him. He loves us, he liberated us, he leads us, he made us a kingdom, he is our King.

John was with the rest of the disciples when they thought that perhaps Jesus would restore the kingdom (Acts 1). But it was not to be, there was something better. He made us a kingdom. Out of every nation and tribe and language he drew some who made him king of their lives and obeyed him of their own free will and of them he made a kingdom, the kingdom of God and we are that kingdom. This kingdom has a single identity though in nation and tribe and language and culture we are very different. But we are all one in Christ Jesus, this is the unifying factor in our divided world and its only hope. In this kingdom we acknowledge a common authority, Jesus is Lord, his rule is within us. He has written his laws in our hearts and in our minds. He leads us. He made us a kingdom and every kingdom has a divine territory. Though it is not yet that universal kingdom, it will be. Researchers tell us that there are more people coming to Christ today than at any time previously in the world's history. Did we but know it we are the alternative society that the world is looking for, and the more we let Jesus lead us the more it will be true.

A Leader in Love

He licenses us, he made up priests. Bishops license men to be priests. Jesus made us priests. This is a strange combination, a kingdom and priests. R. H. Charles says the text just means that Christ has made us a kingdom, each member of which is a priest to God. This is not an original idea. It was first brought out in the time of Moses when he was constituting Israel a nation. They were to be a kingdom of priests (Exodus 19:6). They had been slaves, but he had liberated them. He made them a kingdom, a kingdom of priests. It's a strange idea to our modern way of thinking yet it's quite simple. It means this, no Christian can ever be a dead end. He has something to do for others. He has to bring them to God, he has to bring God to them. That is what a priest does, and God has made us priests by Jesus. Israel forgot this and began to behave exclusively and think that they were the only people. That led to terrible trouble. None of us lives for himself. We have a job to do and there is none higher in the world than to represent men to God in prayer, and represent God to men in witness.

He loves us, he liberated us, he leads us and he licenses us to serve him as priests. We can get right into God and enjoy his presence. It's not surprising that John breaks into praise. 'To him be glory and power for ever and ever.' What does it mean to say, 'To him be glory?' Glory is one of these untranslatable words. Unfortunately in English it is also a word that rolls off the tongue in song and prayer in a way which makes us content with the sound and we never bother to probe for the meaning. That came home to me once when I was reading Patterson's book *The Story of the Churches Song*. He was commenting on that hymn that many of you will know, 'Oh that will be glory for me.' He said that is the absolute nadir or lowest point of unevangelical egotism. That got through to me. It's not about glory for me, it's about glory for him. There are two sides to this New Testament idea of glory. The Greek side has to do with a person's distinctive reputation, 'doxa' is the word. People's opinion about another man is the 'doxa', his reputation. And here John is saying that it is Jesus he wants to get glory. That means he wants him to be recognised for what he is, what he has distinctively done, recognised by as many as possible, recognised by the whole world. When we say or sing to him 'Be glory' it is hypocrisy unless we are making him known so that men recognise him. The Hebrew side of the word is more difficult, mystical. It has to do with that indescribable brightness and unutterable feeling associated when men come close to God. The throne scenes that follow in this book of Revelation give some hint of it. When the Hebrews talked about that something which is more than physical, but which I can't say better than 'glory'. And so the doxology 'To him be glory', is a prayer that all the scales will fall from all human eyes and we shall see him as he is. The predominant feeling in the early Christians under persecution was that sense of powerlessness. But in this book of Revelation Jesus rolled back the curtain and let John see into the unseen. There it was clear that the power was in fact with Jesus. All that was waiting was for that power that was vested in him, the Lamb, to become obvious. That was what John longed for, that Jesus might be seen to rule. And that is our longing too, that the leader we love, who loves us, who liberated us, who licenses us to be priests might come into his own. That men might recognise him for what he is and bow beneath his sway. Is this not a leader to love and worship?

RELEASE FROM OUR PAST

by the Revd. Tom Houston

I want to consider this question about the life of Jacob: 'How did Jacob become Jacob instead of Israel for about sixty years of his life?'

It is common enough for speakers to distinguish between sin and sins. The condition of sin on the one hand and acts of sin on the other. Sometimes it is put this way; sin is the root and sins the fruit. We are quite good at speaking about sins the fruit. But there is not too much spelling out of sin as the root. As I thought about this original sin, I realised that part of it, at least, comes to us from our families. In the ten commandments there is this very serious statement, 'I am the Lord your God, a jealous God visiting the iniquity of the fathers upon the children to the third and fourth generation of those that hate me, but showing steadfast love to thousands of those who love me and keep my commandments.' This implies that part of the burden of sin with which we human beings start comes to us from our families. And this is quite a prominent note in the New Testament. So it seems to me that we have to face up to this in the call to holiness, and Jacob is a case in point, as I hope to show.

First look at the place of his family, in Jacob being Jacob. There are two fixed points in the life story of this man. Two questions that are basically the same but have different answers. Isaac says to Jacob, 'Who are you?' And he replies, 'I am Esau' (Gen. 27:18, 19). And then the man who wrestled with Jacob said, 'What is your name?' And the answer came back, 'I am Jacob.'

So we begin with the family setting. Jacob had a somewhat inadequate father. He was a man lacking in originality, digging up wells that Abraham had dug before, making the same mistakes as his father down in Egypt. His mother, Rebekah, was both good looking and able. She was a winner. They were a long time without children, twenty years in fact, and after very many prayers, it was twins. She had a dreadful pregnancy and often felt ready to die. So much so that she asked God a very painful 'Why is this happening to me?' And she got an impressive answer (25:23). The message from God was that (a) the two children she was carrying would found two nations, and (b) that the elder would serve the younger. There was to be fame for both and the normal order of the primacy of the first born would be set aside and the last would be first. In other words, before Jacob ever came on the scene, there was this prophecy that he would come out on top. It was quite a birth. The first boy was born very red and very hairy, and the second with his little white hand on the red heel of his older twin with a grip that wouldn't let go. It became quite a joke, that little white hand on the red heel. It even made them call the second of the twins, Jacob. Jacob is variously translated as 'you will have found a supplanter', or 'cheat', or in the latest Living

Bible translation as 'grabber'. Notice this, the name was foisted on him. It was a nickname from birth with a family story to go with it. To be brought out on every suitable occasion, and every time re-inforcing the name.

We have one more detail of family background to fill in, a rather tragic detail. In verse twenty-eight we read that Isaac loved Esau because he ate of his venison. But Rebekah loved Jacob. Favouritism in parents is always damaging to children. But it is even more so when the favouritism is based on the fact that the child reinforces a weakness or a prejudice of the parent. A chip off the old block. Isaac liked his food and Esau gave him it the way he liked it. Now add to that the fact that the split between the boys put all the manly virtues on Esau. He was the firstborn with all the rights. And all the softer virtues were given to Jacob. He was paler skinned, smoother of complexion with fine hands, home loving. And you have all the makings of an identity crisis. For Jacob wanted to be Esau and have what Esau had. He wanted his father's favour, he wanted God's blessing that would make him great, and his mother who was a winner egged him on.

Our stage is set for our second point, the false search. Jacob trying to be somebody else. Incident number one had to do with his brother (25:29–34). He had been out hunting and came back famished. Jacob had learned that the 'food game' was important. So he said to himself that two can play at that game. And he withheld food from Esau until he had promised to give him his birth-right, his right to the blessing. That was the grabber mark one.

Grabber mark two had to do with his father. The foolish old man played into the hands of his wife and second son by associating the patriarchal blessing of

God with the life-long indulgence in which he stupidly provided himself. You can't help feeling, when you recognise that he still had eighty years to go, that he was more concerned about a good meal than he was about passing on the blessing. So the one who gave him his food the way he wanted it would get the blessing. But two can play at that game, and Rebekah deceived Isaac, and Jacob got the blessing. The old man is blind and thinks he is failing. 'Who are you my son?' And he had to say, at last, 'I am Esau.' I doubt that he ever wanted to admit that. But Isaac, and the circumstances, made him do it. So he became, for all time, the representative of some of us all the time, and all of us some of the time, when we wish we were somebody else. It happens in families. There are boys who wish they were girls, and there are girls who wish they were boys. There are boys who wish they were brainy or practical or good-looking or whatever, because they feel that their brother or sister gains by being that, or because they feel that's what their father or mother would like. It also happens outside the family, usually because of admiration for one of your own age or set. And it all adds up to this: if you are asked the question 'Who are you?' you don't know. But you would probably choose someone other than yourself if you had to say, and your family will probably have played quite an important part in your uncertainty.

This leads to a familiar syndrome. The man who is trying to be somebody else. And there are three facets to this. It leads to a bargaining relationship with God. We sing the paraphrase 'O God of Bethel', and if you will notice in your hymn books that some have four verses and some have five. The one that has five includes the verse, 'Such blessings from thy gracious hands, our humble prayers implore, and thou shalt be our chosen God, from now to evermore.' Now that's not a Christian prayer, that's a pagan prayer. The Scripture language was this: when God met him, to assure him, as he was running away from his brother, Jacob says to God: 'If you will be with me and do this, and if you will keep me, and if you will give me this, and bring me back, then the Lord shall be my God.' A bargain, and that's dangerous. The gospel begins and ends with what God is, not with what we want or think we need. It is dangerous for the reason that God will not always oblige when you start bargaining in that way, and you may be left with no faith at all if your self-imposed conditions of faith are not met. In other words, if you are going to have a life with God, it has to start with God on his terms, not on yours. But here is this man who is trying to be someone else getting into a bargaining relationship with God. So that syndrome of the person who is trying to be someone else is trying to bring God in to be part of his equipment, to help him do or be what he would like to be. That is not Christian, that is sin.

The second part of the syndrome is strained relationships wih others. First in the family. Esau hated Jacob, and I suppose you say as I would that he had reason to. Trying to be someone else puts a distance between you and other people for you are always acting a part. You are always different inside from what you are out front, and no matter how much you think you are concealing it, people read this instinctively, and relationships become difficult. But this strained relationship was not just with Esau, who might have been regarded as the other main character in the drama. Relationships were difficult in his marriage. You will read about it in chapter twenty-nine, and it is tragic. Someone who is trying to be someone else wants a partner as part of his equipment, and he has very fixed ideas of the kind of wife he wants. She had better be good. And that's the tragedy of Jacob's home. He knew what he wanted, but Leah was foisted on him. Nevertheless, the way he got her is no excuse for treating her the way he did, making her life a misery. God saw that Leah was not loved. And isn't there an irony in the fact that when Jacob gets his ideal wife, she at first cannot have children, and then later dies in childbirth. You can't use people.

The third part of the relationship that went wrong was with his in-laws, Laban. I think the place where it comes most beautifully into focus is where they set up the marker that they called 'Mizpah' (the Lord watch between you and me when we are absent one from the other). These two were such twisters, vying with each other to get the advantage, that they had to put up some kind of religious symbol so that God was watching them when they were trying to get the better of the other. It goes on 'If you ill treat my daughters when I am not there to look after them, God is our witness.' And that story of Laban and Jacob is the story of twenty years scheming and planning, each to outwit the other. When you are in this business of difficult relationships, you sometimes even use a religious front for what you are after.

This syndrome of trying to be someone else leads thirdly to a manipulating use of things. For Jacob, all the time that he was with Laban, his work and his wages were tied up with achieving what he wanted: wives, cattle, power. He was twenty years with Laban building it all up, and he succeeded. But when it came to the crunch, he was equally ready to spend it all in one day, just to appease Esau and get what he wanted.

Release from Our Past

This leads us to the third point in our consideration of Jacob's identity, the final solution (ch. 32). Sooner or later, we have to face up to ourselves as we really are. With Jacob it came years after his first false answer to the question, 'Who are you?' On his way back, he has to face Esau whom he had cheated again. He hears that Esau is coming to meet him with four hundred men, and is scared. What does he do? He disposes of his caravan. And he sacrifices lot after lot of his possessions to buy the favour of his offended twin, sending them on ahead. Finally, he is left by himself on the other side of the brook, and then something happens which he had not bargained for. 'A man wrestled with him' (32:24). All his precautions suddenly became useless. His own life was under threat. And as the bout went on, his thigh was dislocated. He was crippled. And Jacob is aware that somehow God is involved in this terrible struggle. With no power left but to cling, he cries, 'I will not let you go unless you bless me.' He is still the same desperate man, hungry for blessing, hungry for recognition. Why? It had been promised before his birth that Esau had handed the blessing over to him. His father had put his hands on his head and said, 'You have got it.' He had proved it by his success. It seemed as though the blessing was his. But Jacob knew inside that he had obtained this blessing by supplanting, cheating, grabbing – living up to his name. Now he admits it, as he admits his identity before God. What a moment that was for him. What a moment when we admit and accept what we are. What agony, yet what relief. Sickness yielding to health. Deceit yielding to truth. Pride yielding to humility. Striving, endless striving and restlessness yielding to peace, God's peace. And with the swiftness of lightning came the answer, 'You are no more Jacob, but Israel.' The name he resented yet felt forced to live up to, fell away in the light of God. He was a prince. That's what his name means. A limping, halting, humble prince. He had seen God face to face, and in the same moment seen himself. It was a tremendous moment, and as the dawn rose, he found all his fears and precautions were unnecessary. His relationships improved. God gave him favour with Esau, and there was no problem. For the second time in twelve hours he says, 'Truly, to see your face is like seeing the face of God.' The next day when he sees Esau he finds that Esau holds nothing against him. The lonely experience with God in the night is confirmed by the new acceptance of, and by his brother in the day.

He had one son still to be born – eleven of Jacob's children were born before that experience, only one afterwards, and that was Benjamin. It is fascinating to read this story and find that nearly all the other children of Jacob were named by their mother. And Rachel who was dying in childbirth said that this child was to be called Benoi, 'the child of my sorrow.' And for the first time ever, Jacob interfered and said, 'No, he will be Benjamin, the son of my right hand.' No nickname for this boy at birth, no negative ideas to be sewn into the family history to warp him in a direction that is going to take him years to throw off. As Jacob got rid of his own nickname and discovered what God's purpose really was for him, he began to apply it to his own family. So he acts in the light of his release from his past with his post-Peniel son. And then he acts in the light of his release with his grandchildren (v. 48).

The Jacob story is not unique. We are all like him in some respects, for we are all the children of our families yet we all have to find the way God has for us. And there is the tension between what our family disposes us to be and to do, and what new things God has planned for us as his children. Some of this has to do with our character and the battle with sin. Many of the things that we find difficult to triumph over in terms of our Christian behaviour have to do with the things that have been programmed into us by the kind of families we come from, our careers and what work we will do. There are parents who have a set idea as to what their children should be and should do, and becoming a Christian means putting that under the light of the guidance of God and his word.

What am I to say to you? First, it is a problem Jesus had. When he started his public ministry, his mother and brothers thought he was a bit odd. They tried to get him back and cool him down, and there was that estrangement between Jesus and his own mother. He had to find God's way for himself, and it sometimes meant pushing against the ideas the family had. And he said it would be like that for us. That loving him would often come into conflict with loving mother, father, husband, wife, and all that families set up. So I suggest three rules. Please recognise that it is an area that has to be consciously worked at.

The call to holiness is so often battled out in this whole area of family. The troubles in churches that arise from natural families that have never become spiritual families, dominating the scene are legion. So churches are built up of natural families rather than becoming the family of God. Recognise that this is an area that has to be consciously worked at. Secondly, believe in your new inheritance, in your heredity from God. We are, says Peter, partakers of the divine nature. We have been born anew, not of perishable seed but of imperishable. We have the Spirit. The Christian has a new nature, and we need to believe it, and to develop it. There will be a hundred things to make you want to deny it, but believe it, count on the new nature that God gave you in Christ and let it work out day by day, and detail by detail. The third is make good use of the Bible. The Bible was in the first instance the agent of the new birth. We are begotten again by the word of truth, but it is also the agent of the change that needs to come as through our lifetime we become more the children of God and less the children of our parents.

So God made Jacob Israel. He made Simon Peter. He made Saul Paul. And he will make you into another unique example of his grace.

AN ANSWERED PRAYER
(1 Chronicles 4:9, 10)

by the Revd. Gilbert W. Kirby M.A.

I recall my surprise and delight when I stumbled across these two verses tucked away amidst a whole list of unpronounceable names! And since I made that discovery, those two verses have become particularly precious to me.

They relate to a man called Jabez, of whom we know comparatively little. His very name, no doubt, is significant. It means 'sorrowful'. It appears that there were certain distressing circumstances relating to his birth. It may be that his mother died in childbirth; certainly there was some kind of cloud in connection with his coming into the world. But as far as his character was concerned, that is a different story. We are told that 'He was more honourable than his brothers.' This speaks of his own personal devotion. Spiritually he stood out among his contemporaries. Maybe he lived at a time when the spiritual life of the people was at a low ebb, and here was a man who was different. Someone who put the rest of us to shame because of his own upright life and personal devotion, a man of integrity. That is all we are told about Jabez as a person but my main interest in him is because of the prayer he prayed.

We are told that he 'Called on the God of Israel'. In other words, he did not pray to an unknown God but to One with whom he was in covenant relationship. This is the secret of true prayer. We should know the One to whom we address ourselves, the God in whom we have come to put our trust. We may *say* our prayers before we enter God's family, but we only really begin to *pray* when we know God as our Father.

One can learn a great deal from the substance of a man's prayer. It reflects his character, his objectives and aspirations, and it is through his prayer that we come to know this man Jabez. He begins with an earnest plea for personal blessing. We may feel that this is selfish, yet who can be a blessing to others before he has himself first been blessed? There are times in all our lives when we need to come apart with a similar plea. 'Oh that thou wouldest bless me!' It may be that we have fallen away or become depressed; we may have lost our first love for the Lord or our vision for his service. All of us need a deeper knowledge of and love for Christ. We never reach the point when the prayer of Jabez is irrelevant.

From the prayer for personal blessing, Jabez proceeds to ask God to 'Enlarge his border'. It may be originally Jabez meant this in a very literal sense. He needed more land. Possibly some of the land which should have been his was still being occupied by the Canaanites, and he needed God's help in expelling them. Surely, we should be justified in spiritualising such a prayer? For us, 'Enlarge my border' may mean 'Increase my vision, deepen my faith'. Some of us tend to become very parochial in outlook. We think merely in terms of our local scene, and forget that 'The field is

An Answered Prayer

the world.' Some become very wrapped up in their own particular denomination, and rarely see beyond it. The interests of some are limited to their own immediate circle of family and friends. Some get depressed because in their own experience little seems to be happening, and they need to be reminded that God is mightily at work in his world. When a company of people gathers from many parts of the world, it does enable us to gain a wider vision. It can also be a most salutory experience.

The third petition which Jabez made is that God's hand might be with him. He wanted to be sure of God's guiding, controlling presence. He didn't want to step outside God's will for his life. Whenever we are called on to make decisions in our lives how necessary it is that we should know that God's hand is upon us. Moses realised this when he stood on the threshold of the Promised Land and prayed, 'If Thy presence will not go with me, do not carry us up from here.'

How important it is, not only for young Christians, but for us all, that we should not first make our plans and then seek God's blessing for them. But rather pray for guidance before we commit ourselves.

The fourth and final petition in the prayer of Jabez was that he might be kept from harm or evil. Here is a man who did not underestimate the power of the enemy. He was acutely conscious of what he was up against. He knew, perhaps from bitter experience, the effect of stepping outside the will of God. We, too, need to know what we face. We are up against a ruthless and skilful enemy who is always ready to attack us, and we need God's keeping power if we are not to be hurt in the battle. Did not our Lord himself teach his disciples to pray, 'Lead us not into temptation'? We can be kept from hurt and harm but only by the power of God.

Keswick Seventysix

There is much we can learn from this brief prayer of Jabez. There were no wasted words. It was straight to the point. It was a prayer that touched on realities in his life. How comforting it is to us to learn that 'God granted what he asked.' We would do well, at a time like this to make the prayer of Jabez our own. And if we do, we can be confident that it is the sort of prayer that God will be well pleased to answer.

THE SECRET OF PEACE
(Romans 6)

by the Revd. Gilbert W. Kirby M.A.

In his letter to the Romans the Apostle Paul has been dealing, up till now (ch. 6), with the subject of justification. He has shown that the ground of our justification in the sight of God is solely on the groud of God's grace, for example, 'Since all have sinned and fall short of the glory of God, they are justified by his grace as a gift through the redemption which is in Christ Jesus' (3:23, 24). Justified by God's free grace, his unmerited favour to us sinners. Then he goes on to point out that our sole means of justification is our faith (3:28). Then as we turn to chapter five, we find that the outcome of our justification is that we have peace with our God through our Lord Jesus Christ. All that follows a pattern which is to do with our standing in the sight of God. But from there the Apostle proceeds to use a technical term. The doctrine of sanctification. How we are to go on with the Lord and live the Christian life. So that is where we have alighted at chapter six.

God is doing remarkable things today in many parts of the world, including our own country. Thousands of

Keswick Seventysix

people are being converted. But everywhere I go I hear the same cry, 'They must be taught, they need teaching.' And I think this is very true because although many people have accepted Christ as their Saviour, they don't know much about where they go from there. They know about the historic facts, the fact that Christ died and rose again, but they don't know the deeper meaning of those historic facts. Well, there is nothing new about that situation. Paul was dealing with a similar situation. He was dealing with the kind of person who might say in ignorance, 'Are we to continue in sin that grace may abound?' After all, you have told us that we are saved by grace through faith so we might as well go on sinning and we will experience more of God's grace. And believe it or not there have been supposed Christians who have argued like that. One of them was a very famous man called Rasputin, a Russian Monk. He did the most terrible things and claimed that the more wickedness he perpetrated, the more he could experience God's forgiveness. But you don't have to think of a man like that. You and I know people, perhaps ourselves, who have excused themselves by saying that we've only got to confess it, and it will all be all right, God is forgiving. But did Paul have to say to people who spoke with such ignorance, 'Are we to continue in sin that grace may abound? God forbid'. It is unthinkable.

The Apostle proceeds to make a statement. But before he does so he asks two further questions. 'How can we who died to sin still live in it? Don't you know that all of us who have been baptised into Christ Jesus were baptised into his death?' In other words, it is incompatible when you think what has happened to us. Life in sin co-exists with death. This brings us back to the question, 'What really happened when we became

The Secret of Peace

Christians?' In the early Church when people believed they were immediately baptised. That may not be customary now, but they certainly did not have baptismal classes or anything of that nature. They were converted, they turned to God, and they were baptised there and then. This was an outward sign that they had entered upon the Christian life. But they were also baptised into Christ, says Paul. They were baptised into his death. Now what did he mean by that? As surely as Christ died on the cross, so did they die to sin at their conversion and subsequent baptism. The verb in verse two, 'We who die to sin', is in a tense known as the aorist and it suggests a single completed past act. So the Apostle asks, how can we go on living in something we've died to. What Paul is calling all Christians to do is to identify themselves with Christ in his death, his burial and his resurrection.

Sometimes in our ignorance we think that a Christian is somebody who has signed a card as a decision for Christ. But there is much more to it than that. 'A Christian by faith inwardly, and by baptism outwardly, has been united to Christ in his death and resurrection,' writes John Stott. Christ's death was a death to sin. He had finished on the cross with all that had to do with sin, and his resurrection was a resurrection to God. That is what being a Christian is. And if you see it that way you will never ask the question, 'Are we to continue in sin that grace may abound?' However, it does not mean that because we are Christians we no longer face temptation. It does not mean that our old sinful nature is eradicated. Paul obviously realised this or he would not have written later on in the same chapter, 'Do not yield your members to sin as instruments of wickedness.'

What does it mean then when it says we have died to

sin. It means that we have died to all that the old life meant and a new life has begun. The last thing that a Christian ought to be is to be enslaved to sin in any form whatsoever. Our birthright as believers is to be set free from bondage to sin. What was crucified with Christ is the man I once was, my old unregenerate self, my pre-conversion life. And that is what we have got to tell people when they become Christians. Don't be superficial in our preaching of the gospel. Tell people that it is as drastic as that. We have, however, to play our part, and there are three things that we must never do, if we are going to live a victorious Christian life. First, we must never excuse sin. We must never claim extenuating circumstances. Secondly, we must never excite sin. You know yourself and you know what will excite sin in you. If you really want to be victorious you must never place yourself in a particularly vulnerable position whereby you excite sin. And never expect to sin, expect to be victorious. Never expect failure, claim victory.

All that I have said so far has been negative, but it is a necessary side to the picture. But the other side is positive. Not only are we identified with Christ in his death but we are identified with Christ by faith in his resurrection. We are to walk in newness of life. 'If any man is in Christ,' says the Scriptures, 'he is a new creation.' A new person, people that are unrecognisable because they are in Christ Jesus. Now what does it mean? Being a Christian means so very much more than some of us realise, especially if we were converted when we were young. It means that as a Christian I have new standards of conduct. Every aspect of my life is affected and I am to walk in newness of life. This affects my home, my school, my work place, my standards of

The Secret of Peace

honesty, integrity and truthfulness. The whole of life is affected. New standards of conduct means a new outlook on life. The world has been crucified, says Paul. The world crucified to me and I to the world. I am afraid that some Christians haven't caught that yet. They are still in the 'rat race'. They still covet anything and everything that this world can offer, they still try to keep up with the Joneses. That is not your mentality as a believer. You have a new outlook on life. You are no longer wrapped up in material possessions, they are second rate to you now, or they should be. You have a new motivation. The non-Christian is out to please himself. He may do it in a nice way but that is what he is out to do. What is your motivation as a Christian? That you may please the Lord Jesus Christ. You have a new social concern. Paul wrote to the Philippians, 'Look not every man on his own interests but on the interests of others.' You are not just concerned about your well being, you are concerned about your neighbour. You are to consider yourself as having been raised from the dead to walk in newness of life with an entirely new outlook, a new attitude, a new aspiration. A verse in this chapter that impresses me reads, 'Now that you have been set free from sin and have become slaves of God' (v. 22). That is what we should be as Christians, and the return we get is sanctification and its end is eternal life.

I think we ought to ask ourselves some basic questions: Have I really grasped what it is to be a Christian? Did I think it was a sort of easy believism? Do I realise how drastic it is, and consider myself dead to sin and alive to God, set free from sin's dominion and becoming now a slave of righteousness, a slave of God? That is what you are called to my brothers and sisters, nothing less than that. To what extent are my members yielded to God? Paul says here, 'Do not yield your members to sin as instruments of wickedness, but yield yourselves to God as men who have been brought from death to life and your members to God as instruments of righteousness.'

Have you yielded your members, talents, personality, spiritual or natural gifts to God? Maybe this is the moment for us to face reality. Are we going to recognise that not only has Christ died for us but that we have died in him. And as he died and rose again so we have died and we are to be identified with him in resurrection life. That is true Christianity.

PRELUDE TO VICTORY
(Mark 14:32 – 42)

by Alan Nute

'And they went to a place which was called Gethsemane . . . ' Jesus bends quietly over the recumbent forms of his three favoured disciples. Sheer exhaustion, both physical and emotional, has proved just too much for them and they have surrendered at length to the overwhelming need for sleep. Gently, he rouses them. And I seem to hear some pathos in his voice as he speaks to them, 'Could you not watch with me one hour?' The spirit is willing, but the flesh is weak. Eventually, their slumbers are penetrated as the voice of Jesus comes to them urgently bidding them to rise and to go with him for the betrayer had come. Verse forty-three informs us that immediately Judas came with a crowd with swords and clubs from the chief priests and elders. Simon Peter probably said to himself, 'Well at least I'm prepared. I'm not going to allow them to arrest him without a struggle.' He had anticipated trouble, so he had armed himself with a sword. He reaches for that sword and slashes the nearest person to him, who happened to be a member of the High Priest's band, but all he manages to do is to sever the young fellow's ear. Judged from some standpoints it was a brave action. After all, he and the others were hopelessly outnumbered and the enemy was armed to the teeth. Impulsive, it might have been, but nevertheless it was a bold and brave thing to do. On the other hand, it was misguided. It was a dangerous thing to do. It could so easily have precipitated a battle there in the garden. More important than that, the action was out of keeping with the spirit of Jesus and with the will of the Father. The arm that wielded the sword was the arm of flesh, and the flesh was weak. But don't let's censor Peter too severely, for our deeds must often have caused embarrassment to our Lord.

Quite different from Peter is the annonymous youth who is also described for us (vv. 51, 52), 'A young man followed him with nothing but a linen cloth about his body, and they seized him, but he left the linen cloth and ran away naked.' There is a fascinating conjecture that this youth was none other than John Mark. However that may be, we are faced here with a courageous action. This young fellow, whoever he was, determined to stay with his Lord to the end. Is there any counterpart to that in your experience? Vows of allegiance. Determination to follow Christ to the end. And then a moment of crisis and we deny our Lord. We can identify with Peter and this unnamed youth – and the verdict is that the spirit indeed is willing, but the flesh is weak.

What a contrast Jesus presents. Watch him as he emerges from the shadows of Gethsemane. In his face is steadfastness, in his bearing a quiet dignity. A determination marks his every step, and when he speaks, his words are deliberately chosen. He utters them without passion, and when the enemy would provoke him to a

Prelude to Victory

rash outburst he remains silent. Here is one who is in perfect control. All that his disciples, and I so often add, I would not be. Their defeat, his triumph, are both traceable to what transpired in the garden. For Jesus, Gethsemane was the prelude to victory. First, our Lord Jesus confessed confidence in God. Jesus foresaw in that hour the horror of great darkness that was about to engulf him. He glimpsed the desolation which was to be his, because he, who knew no sin, was going to be made sin for us. At that moment, he makes this great confession. 'Abba, Father, all things are possible to thee.' Earlier in his ministry he prayed, 'Father, Lord of heaven and earth' as though he would with one hand take a fresh grip on his relationship with God as he addresses him as 'Father', and with the other hand upon his power, 'Lord of heaven and earth'. He steadies his soul for the conflict as he appropriates these two great facts of God's fatherhood, and of his divine omnipotence. The words are intimate, personal, trustful, affectionate. And linked with that, 'All things are possible to thee.'

Now if he, the only Son of the Father, should make this confession, how much more should we? Aware of what we might regard almost as an unequal struggle, shall we not cry out in a confident assertion, 'Abba, Father, all things are possible to thee.'

Abraham had been challenged with the words 'Is anything too hard for the Lord?' Job confessed, 'I know that thou canst do all things,' and Jeremiah, 'Nothing is too hard for thee.' Gabriel had asserted this to Mary, 'With God, all things are possible.' And Jesus had prayed it. May I ask, do you doubt it? If you do, come with me and watch reverent hands take that sacred body down from the tree and bear it away for burial. And they place it in the cold of Joseph's tomb. Locked in that sepulchre are the forlorn hopes of the disciples. Abandoned for ever. The stone is sealed and the guard set. And all the dark fields of hell group around that sepulchre to withstand the resurrection that he had promised. But three days later we visit that tomb. The guards have fled, the seal is broken, the stone is removed, and the grave is vacant. We turn and Jesus greets us, risen from the tomb.

But here is a second factor in the prelude to triumph. Christ says, 'Remove this cup from me, yet not what I will, but what thou wilt.' This was his deliberate commitment to God. To his acknowledged dependence, Jesus now adds 'Remove this cup from me'. His humanity was no sham. The desire not to experience the bitterness of that cup was natural, and the expression of that desire was completely genuine. But over-riding that desire was the supreme desire for the will of God to be done. It was that that he chose. We should not feel guilty if we also tremble and hesitate as we face the will of God. For the will of God can be a costly thing. Obeying it may demand the surrender of some cherished ambition, or the yielding up of some enjoyed friendship, things which might be weights impending our spiritual progress. The cost is great and your strength is small, and all the time your heart echoes the words 'Remove this cup from me.' But can you add these vital words, 'Not what I will, but what thou will?' The power is his, but the response is yours.

And so I ask, what was it that made for the startling contrast between the Lord and his disciples in those scenes that follow Gethsemane? His path of triumph resulted from his confessed confidence in God, his deliberate commitment to God, and thirdly, his purposeful

Prelude to Victory

communion with God. And this is the third factor in this prelude to victory. Just as its omission was largely the cause of his disciples' defeat. Watch and pray for on this hangs the issue of the day. It is here that the battle is really lost or won. And yet, critical though the occasion was for Jesus, this was not an emergency prayer time. Such communion was the habit of his life. Often his disciples had seen him slip away in the early morning to a quiet place with his Father. The Saviour's triumph may be traced to the prayer conflict in the garden, and further to the many times he had resorted thither. That prayer conflict was costly. J. Oswald Sanders observes in one of his essays that Jesus performed many mighty works without outward sign of strain. But of his praying it is recorded that he offered up prayers and supplications with loud cries and tears. The three strands which combine in the experience of our Lord Jesus and which must be in ours too if we are to follow him in the path of victory are: 1. A confessed confidence in God. 2. A deliberate commitment to God. 3. A purposeful communion with God.

A LIVING SACRIFICE
(Romans 12:1, 2)

by the Revd. G. Osei-Mensah

Many of us know enough truth to be converted, but we do not know enough of the truth of God to be able to stand confidently against the evil one when he comes to attack us, tempt us, and lead us astray. Even when we want to do the Lord's will, we hardly know how to define that will. So we fumble our way, and before long we find ourselves back in sin. Paul has described in his letter to the Romans the doctrines of grace, the teaching of what God has done for them, before going on to tell them what kind of consistent life they ought to live. He pauses at these two verses and makes an appeal on the basis of what he has already taught, and in preparation for all that he was going on to expound to them. So he was begging them to give themselves wholly to Christ, to let him rule their moral lives, control their affections and ambitions, so that they may know the victory that comes through a surrendered life.

If a Hebrew wanted to bring an offering to the Lord he would take either from the flock or, if he was poor, two turtle doves. But in any case he would bring the animal to the priest, and lay his hand upon the animal and the priest would slaughter the animal. The blood of the animal would be poured beside the altar and the animal cut piece by piece. The entrails and legs would be washed clean in water and then the pieces of the animal would be put upon the altar. The whole animal would be consumed to ashes. As the smoke ascended we are told that it was a pleasing odour for the Lord, a fragrant offering by fire. One of the few offerings where no part of the animal is eaten either by priest or worshipper. And that is the kind of picture that the Apostle is using here as a living sacrifice.

In calling it a living sacrifice he presents three contrasts with the ordinary burnt offering. (1) It is a living sacrifice of our bodies, and not animal substitutes. (2) It is living bodies that we are to offer, not a corpse. There are some in Africa who join the church for the sole reason that they want a Christian burial. That is not the kind of sacrifice the Lord is looking for. He is not looking for a corpse, he is looking for a living body. We are to present our bodies, a living sacrifice. (3) God is not interested in empty ceremonies or rituals. What God wants is our spiritual worship, which the A.V. translates 'Our reasonable service'. That means an intelligent response to the love of God with our whole heart and our wills. That is the picture the Apostle presents. Offering ourselves a living sacrifice, holy and acceptable to God.

Now I would like to answer two questions. Why should we offer ourselves sacrificially to the Lord in this way? Why should we submit ourselves so totally and completely to the Lord? What reasons does the Apostle give for us to do this kind of thing? And secondly, what does it mean in practice to offer ourselves a living sacrifice, acceptable to God? Why should we submit ourselves to the Lord in this way? There are two reasons. The first one you will find at the end of chapter eleven. 'For of him, and through him, and to him, are all things; to whom be glory for ever. Amen.' That is the reason why you should offer yourself completely to him. He is the source of everything and he is the source of you. He made you. He has the right by creation; we came forth from him, he made us. From him are all things. Through him are all things. The Apostle says, 'In him we live and move and have our being.' The Lord is our sustainer and that is the reason why we should give ourselves wholly to him, he has our very breath in his hands. But he also says, 'To him are all things.' He is our proper destination and we will never know fulfilment of the personalities he made us to be unless we are prepared to offer ourselves to him.

The second reason why we should offer ourselves is that we belong to God by right of his redemption. I believe we are the weaker spiritually and morally when we do not take enough time to meditate upon the mercies of God. We do not marvel at it until the power of this new affection drives away all other affections. Until we begin to love him as he has loved us. 'By the mercies of God.' What are the mercies of God? He made us alive together with Christ when we were dead in trespasses and sins. Think of the cost. 'God so loved the world that he gave his only begotten Son.' He had only one Son and he gave him up for us. That is how much it cost God to love us. And we are told by Isaiah that 'He was wounded for our transgressions, he was bruised for our iniquities ... it was the will of his father to bruise him ... he made his soul an offering for sin.' That's how much the mercies of God cost him. I appeal to you by the mercies of God. Think how utterly un-

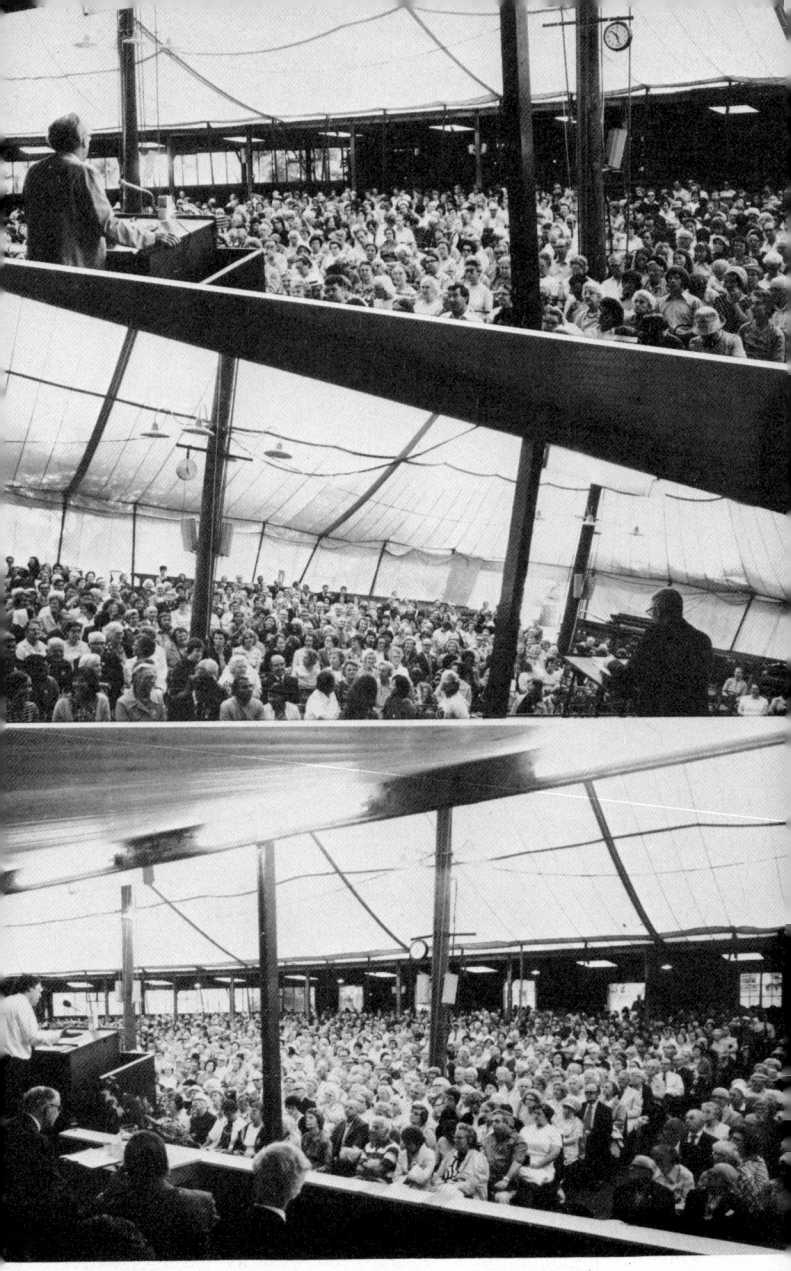

Speakers in action: George Duncan, Alan Neech, Eric Alexander

(*Top to bottom, L to R*) Gordon Bridger, Alan Neech, Tom Houston, Peter Gompertz, John Caiger, Michael Cole, Maurice Wood, Godfrey Osei-Mensah, Alan Redpath

(*Top to bottom*, *L to R*) A. Skevington-Wood, Alan Nute, Eric Alexander, George Duncan, Alec Motyer, Gilbert Kirby, A. T. Houghton, Derek Prime, Herbert Cragg

First week speakers and committee members (*Standing L to R*) Deryck Thompson, W. C. L. Filby, Derek Prime, Kenneth Habershon, D. N. Carr, E. R. Appleton, Gordon Bridger, M. N. W. Burch, H. W. Cragg, G. E. Dunning, H. G. Wheeler, (*Sitting L to R*) Alan Redpath, Harry Sutton, J. A. Caiger, A. S. Neech, A. T. Houghton, M. A. P. Wood, T. F. C. Bewes, A. Skevington Wood, G. B. Duncan.

A Living Sacrifice

deserved we are of these mercies, 'For God commended his love to us while we were yet sinners.' Think how entirely adequate it is. He assures us there is nothing he will withhold from us. It is your spiritual worship, it is your intelligent response to all his mercies, his costly mercies, your undeserved mercies and his adequate mercies. Paul is calling for a total submission of ourselves to our Lord Jesus Christ. He tells us that he is worthy of this submission. It is reasonable that we do this. As moral beings we must submit to his right to rule our moral lives and choices. This is where we find it hardest. It is very easy to accept forgiveness of sins from the merciful hands of God, but when he asserts his right as Lord to determine our moral choices, then we are not as forthcoming. But this is what he requires of us. If we call him Lord we must crown him Lord here also. As intelligent beings we are to submit our minds to be taught and renewed by the Spirit with the word. The renewing of our minds, we are told, is the work of the Spirit. He brought us to birth and he renews our minds in the likeness of the One who created us. He challenges our thinking, he takes away the concepts which we have inherited from the world. He purges our minds of all the things that are wrong, all the things that are unreal and he teaches us the eternal truth of God.

Paul sums it up earlier on in this same letter. 'Do not yield your members to sin as instruments of wickedness, but yield yourselves to God as men and women who have been brought from death to life and your members to God as instruments of righteousness' (6:13). That is what is consistent with all the mercies of God that have been shown to us. He then goes on to tell us that if we do this it will involve us in two things. It will mean tearing ourselves away from the world and its false values and desires. Instead we are to turn to the will of God and seek it with all our might and with all the resources that are given to us. Making that the control of our lives. Do not be conformed to this world, be transformed by the renewing of your mind. Don't let the world force you into its mould. Don't let the world push you into its fashion, attitudes and values. Let the Lord Jesus Christ by the work he has already done in your heart change the whole of your outlook on life as you love the things that he loves, as his Spirit works in your heart with his word. He says if we do this then we will prove in our own life and experience what is the good acceptable and perfect will of God for us.

What does it mean in practice? He works this out in three areas. It means holiness for us should be more important than happiness. That means that we must take time to study the Scriptures. We cannot excuse ourselves for not knowing the will of our God. It is plain that we cannot obey his will unless we know it. And it is also plain that unless we take the trouble to find out where he has made his will known, we are not going to know it. And if we are not going to know it then we are not going to do it. It also means that we should take time to cultivate the friendship of our God in prayer. He is in our hearts, we are told by Scripture. But is he locked up somewhere in a little back room? Do we cultivate his friendship? To cultivate the friendship of our Lord means self-discipline. We must allow the Spirit to teach us the things that are of him, allowing him to deal with us, working in our wills to do our Lord's good pleasure. It means a new attitude to ourselves. If we are going to give ourselves to him as a living sacrifice, he is going to teach us many things about ourselves, he is going to help us evaluate ourselves properly (v. 3). There will be

A Living Sacrifice

no room for pride. But neither will there be room for self-pity or false modesty. If we are his he has given us some gift and our business is to discover it, to develop it, and place it at his disposal. It will also change our attitude to the Church. We will now begin to think of fellowship in terms of the body of which we are a member. We will accept our duty in the body. He will accept the discipline of belonging and we will respect the gifts of other people as well as our own. We are told that we are many members but the same body. And that body has only one purpose, to grow up into Christ's likeness, to encourage one another to love and good works. He said it would affect our attitude to the world. We will find ourselves as he commissioned us, light and salt. We will find ourselves making all sorts of research, to see how we can influence men in society for Christ. How we can arrest the decay in society. There is nothing spiritual about sitting in 'holy huddles' and condemning the world outside. We are the salt. If the world is rotting, whose fault is it? Our attitude to the world will change. Our attitude to the fellowship of the church will change. Our attitude to ourselves will change, if we are prepared to submit ourselves to the Lord Jesus Christ and to the authority of his word and Spirit.

I appeal to you by the mercies of God they are adequate, present your bodies to him as a living sacrifice, holy and acceptable to God. It is your spiritual worship. It is your reasonable service. It is your intelligent response, to all that God is and has done for us.

GOD'S SEARCHING QUESTIONS (Gen. 3:1-15)

by the Revd. G. Osei-Mensah

God's searching questions to the first three human beings, Adam, Eve and Cain, reveal something of the nature of sin and God's attitude to it. 'Where are you?' God asked Adam, because Adam was not where God expected him to be. He was not in a right relationship with his Lord. He was not responding to God's friendship. Sin alienates us from the Lord. And Adam's reply indicates the fruit of his actions as he saw them, 'I was afraid because I was naked and I hid myself.' But God's further probe of Adam exposed a root cause as God saw it, disobedience, a rejection of God's authority and truthfulness. The Lord in his authority commanded out of loving wisdom that they should not eat of this fruit.

Adam's reaction showed that sin affects every department of our personality. He said he was ashamed. And a sense of shame was a natural reaction of a moral being who is estranged from God. God who is the true reference of our personality; the point of reference of our dignity and self-respect. Adam was also afraid. And that

God's Searching Questions

shows the insecurity that sin introduces to the human soul. When Satan comes to tempt us to independence and autonomy, he succeeds in making us insecure. God is the reference point of our security. And when Adam was cut off from God he was afraid.

Thirdly, he began to blame his wife. The wife concerning whom he had just been singing a doxology. Now he turns, because of sin, and blames God for giving Eve to him, 'The woman whom you gave to be with me, she is at fault.' The Lord has made us as social beings, but as soon as we sin not only is the relationship with God impaired but also our relationship with one another. Those are some of the things that were revealed by this question that the Lord put to Adam.

God also put a question to Eve, 'What is this that you have done?' he asked; although it is as much an exclamation as a question. There is a naïvety about sin which is tragic. The woman saw that it was good for food, that it was a delight to the eye, and it was desirable to make one wise. Sin will always come like that to us; it seems as though we see but we do not. The deceitfulness of sin blinded her to the forest fire that she had carelessly lit and the consequences of which were beyond her ability to extinguish. Eve means the mother of mankind, by her disobedience she became the murderer of all mankind for all of us are now born with a bias for sin, 'By that one man's disobedience all are made sinners.' There is a warning here for all of us, our sins will reach out far beyond us to other people as well.

The third question God put to Cain, 'Where is Abel your brother?' (Gen. 4:9). And Cain with his hands still red with the blood of Abel scornfully replied, 'Am I my brother's keeper?' And in that reply he actually announced a truth, for the Lord teaches that we are our brother's keeper. In Matthew (5:21, 26) he taught that if we cherish anger in our hearts it is like murder before God who judges our intentions as well as our acts. Also in Matthew (18:6) the Lord Jesus Christ warned that 'Whoever causes one of these little ones who believe in me to sin, it would be better for him to have a great millstone fastened around his neck and be drowned in the depths of the sea.' Paul, when writing to the Corinthians, said that a carelessness and selfish attitude to our appetites, and even to do things that we like and which are legitimate, may in some circumstances be harmful to our brethren. In this case we are not to lock ourselves up into ourselves but we are to have our eyes also on the things that belong to others.

However, these searching questions of God not only reveal the nature of sin, but a way of mercy. We are told three things that the Lord did in the case of these first three human beings. God never pronounces judgement or a warning, without pointing the way of escape. In the midst of the judgement the Lord says this to the enemy of their soul, 'I will put enimity between you and the woman and between your seed and her seed. He shall bruise your head and you shall bruise his head.' And there we have the very first promise of the deliverer whom the Lord was to send. Meanwhile he made provision for the effective covering of their shame by providing garments of skin. Such is God's love that to those who will look to him as their deliverer he not only relieves their conscience of guilt, but clothes them with robes of righteousness.

Towards the end of the third chapter there is also a reference to protection from eternal ruin. And the Lord said, 'Behold man has become like us, knowing good and evil. And now lest he put forth his hand and take also of the tree of life and eat and live forever . . . ' the Lord sent man from the garden of Eden. He drove man out, and that was an act of mercy. In his judgements God always shows mercy. His long suffering and patience is meant to lead us to repentance.

'PETER WAS BLAMED'
(Galatians 2:1 - 21)

by the Revd. Derek Prime, M.Th.

'Peter was to be blamed' or, 'Cephas stood condemned' (RSV). The word used here for *condemn* or *blame* implies that Peter stood condemned by his own action. Suddenly, Peter found himself exposed. He was found out. Something bad in him was brought to light and there was nothing Peter could say in his own defence. And although the context and the sin were very different, Peter's position was not unlike that of the woman taken in the very act of adultery and brought before the Lord Jesus. Because Peter, like her, had nothing to say. Here we are presented with something of a *surprise*.

Think for a moment of who Peter was. He was an Apostle, one of the twelve chosen, called and sent forth by the Lord Jesus himself. Peter had been a witness of the resurrection of the Lord Jesus, and in a marked sense he knew the anointing and the power of the Holy Spirit. The Holy Spirit had led Peter and his fellow Apostles into all truth. His ministry had been confirmed by countless miracles. Yet, at this particular moment,

Peter was Blamed

he was to be blamed. Peter was one of the pillars of the early Church and if you look in verse nine that is how Paul describes him. It is true that immediately prior to the crucifixion Peter had fallen into the snare of self-confidence, and had given way to fear of man. But Peter had been fully restored. He had had an interview with the Lord Jesus when three times the Lord had asked whether Peter loved him. And Peter had affirmed his love. Then he had been recommissioned to feed the flock. The Lord had taught Peter one particular lesson, that the flock extended beyond the Jewish people.

Later Peter in a trance saw a great sheet in which there were all kinds of animals, reptiles and birds. And there came a voice, 'Peter, rise up and eat.' Peter said, 'No Lord, I have never eaten anything that is common or unclean.' And a voice came to him a second time, 'What God has cleansed you must not call common.' The lesson, of course, was that Gentiles, although regarded as unclean by the Jews, were equally to be made clean by the blood of Christ and made acceptable to God. Peter was to accept them as brothers and sisters in the Lord Jesus. Later Peter visited Antioch and sat down at table with Gentile believers, the Lord had taught him that and he enjoyed their hospitality. In turn he was treated as a member of their families. Then suddenly some Jews arrived from James in Jerusalem and Peter guessed that they might not share his understanding of God's revelation concerning the Gentiles, so he cut himself off from close fellowship with the Gentile believers. The greatest commandment is 'That we should love the Lord our God with all our heart and soul and mind', and the second is 'That we should love our neighbour as ourself.' And Peter broke the first great Commandment. He put the fear of man before the fear of God. He broke the second great Commandment in that he treated his fellow believers in a way that he would never have had anyone treat him.

Furthermore, he sinned against his knowledge of the truth. He knew that God looks upon men's hearts, not upon their outward appearance, not where they were born, not the colour of their skin, not their culture, but upon their hearts. And Peter was building up again the very things that God had shown him he must tear down. And Peter knew, full well that everything that does not come from faith is sin. And his action in withdrawing from the Gentiles was not an act of faith, it was an act of disobedience. And Peter was to be blamed, Peter the Apostle.

As we think of Peter's background and privileges, we may be surprised at Peter. But we share the same nature as Peter. No matter how long you have been a Christian, no matter what position you hold in the service of God and in the Church of God, your flesh is as weak today as ever it has been. I suggested that Peter's sin was a *surprise*. I would like now to show you that it was a *disaster*, because as soon as Peter took this step his own fellowship with God was spoiled. Fellowship with the people of God, and fellowship with God himself go hand in hand. Satan may try and tell me otherwise, but I cannot be knowingly in a wrong relationship with the people of God through my sin, and at the same time be in a right relationship with God. Peter's own heart must have condemned him. None could have guessed by looking at Peter what was happening, but Peter knew. And if Peter hadn't recognised it at once, God knew. Peter became a hypocrite. Paul comments in verse thirteen, 'And the other Jews dissembled likewise with him' (A.V.), or, 'With him the rest of the Jews acted insin-

Peter was Blamed

cerely' (RSV). His action in withdrawing from his Gentile brethren, was not a sincere action. But worse still, Peter caused others to stumble. Verse thirteen tells us that not only did other Jews act insincerely following Peter's lead but Barnabas also was carried away with their dissimulation. When a big tree falls in a forest lots of little trees fall with it.

But the greatest aspect of the *disaster* was that Peter obscured the truth of the Gospel. Paul puts his finger on it. 'I saw,' he says, 'that they walked not uprightly according to the truth of the Gospel' (v. 14). My receiving of the Lord Jesus as Saviour and Lord demands a new kind of conduct which pleases God. Peter was dishonouring his Lord who had died for Jew and Gentile, and that threatened to hinder the effective preaching of the gospel. Peter was to be blamed.

Fortunately, that is not the end. It was a situation that was not beyond remedy. We don't know how it worked out in Peter's case, but we do know this that God raised up a brother who spoke the truth to Peter. Paul had to rebuke Peter in front of them all. And will you notice that Peter is not recorded as having made any answer. In fact the word *blamed*, or *condemned*, would seem to imply that he was condemned by his own conscience. What Paul said Peter knew to be true. But if Peter was to be blamed and was rebuked, he was not unloved. God the Father loved him as a son and Peter was restored. But first had to accept the blame. Like Job, Peter had to say, 'I abhor myself, I repent in dust and ashes.' I use that word *abhor* because it is the same word in the Greek that Paul uses here for the word *blame*. Peter was to be blamed. Peter came to the point where he despised and abhorred himself and then God lifted him up and restored him. I want to say this, Peter was to be blamed, but what of us? Are there *surprising* failures in our lives?

I want to end with this note. Thank God, the situation is not beyond remedy. The grace of the Lord Jesus that first brought me forgiveness is the grace that heals backsliding. He gives more grace. He gives it not to the proud, but to the humble and it was in the position of the humble that Peter found it. Peter was to be blamed. He gives more Grace.

LIVING IN THE LIGHT OF HIS RETURN
(Philippians 2)

by the Revd. Dr. Alan Redpath

Out of the twenty-seven books in the New Testament, twenty-three of them make definite and specific reference to the coming again of Jesus. This tremendous truth is the whole emphasis and burden of the book. The hope of Jesus coming again was the inspiration of the early Church, and motivated them as they went out in witness of Christ. It was the burning passion of their lives, the powerful motive for holy living. The hope that Jesus would come soon. How would you define hope? The best definition I can give is, 'expectation plus desire'. I mean, you might expect to get the sack from your job next week, but you don't desire it. You might desire to get a rise in salary next week, but you don't expect it. But when you link expectation with desire, you've got hope. And it was a tremendous living hope that Jesus would come again.

The letter to the Philippians is no exception. I've called it, 'Songs in the Night'. It's really a love letter from Paul to the people of Philippi – and there's no rebuke in it, it is all love; a message of comfort to those who are having a rough time. Paul himself is in prison and suffering. Yet nineteen times in this letter we find the word 'joy' and 'rejoice'. Like a song in the night Paul's message of love and joy comes through the trials. The secret of that joy is that Jesus is coming soon, and there is a phrase that over and over again occurs in this letter, 'the day of Christ'. They are all anticipating the day when Jesus shall come and I believe there was never a time in history when we needed a revival of that hope in our hearts more than we do today. Hope in his coming again has tremendous implications for our witness for Christ and a tremendous impact on our desire for holy living.

This great phrase which recurs in the letter to the Philippians, 'the day of Christ'. First in chapter one verse six, where there is the power for holy living, the total action of the grace of God upon my heart until he comes again. He will work at bringing what he began in my heart to full completion right until the day when he comes back, undeterred by any changing circumstances, undeterred by my stubbornness and waywardness, undismayed by Satanic opposition and unmoved by my temporary coldness. He himself will complete and perfect in me what he began. He created in you and in me the initial desire for himself, and he will mature that character until he is able to say one day about everyone of us, 'I have finished the work which thou gavest me to do.'

But the growth of a Christian is not automatic. We sometimes hear people say that a particular Christian is growing old. No Christian grows old. He becomes old because he doesn't grow and you can become old like that when you are merely thirty. You become stale and dry and cold and dead because of failing to grow. And

Living in the Light of His Return

for this reason a Christian living in the light of Jesus' return has no room for idols in his heart. He will be absolutely abandoned to the purpose of God for his life, and that great purpose is to make us each one like Jesus. As Paul says, 'I press on to lay hold of and make my own that for which he laid hold of me and made me his own. That great goal that God has for me I will make absolutely my goal for myself' (3:12, Phillips). An idol is anything that would threaten the sovereignty of Jesus, his right to rule every moment of my life. Therefore I will make the goal that he has set out for me to be my goal, and we must do the same if we are to live in the light of his return.

The second thing is in verses nine and ten of chapter one – not only the power for a holy life, but the pattern for it. The result of an intelligent love in our hearts will be that God gives us a right sense of values and priorities. That means being sincere, without flaw, testing everything and never causing offence to other people, right up to the day of his return. So a Christian living in the light of eternity not only has no room for idols in his heart, but he has no room for slackness in his service. First in intensity, first in desire, first in preference, all a question of right priorities.

The third reference to that day of Christ is, 'Do all things without grumbling or questioning, that you may be blameless and innocent children of God without blemish in the midst of a crooked and perverse generation, among whom you shine as lights in the world, holding fast the word of Life, so that in the day of Christ I may be proud that I did not run in vain, nor labour in vain' (2:14–16). Here is the motive for holy living in the day of Christ. Do all things without grumbling or questioning, for Jesus is coming soon. The children of Israel were always grumbling in the wilderness, grumbling about their diet and their leadership, longing for the good old days. And we have many people in our churches who are always grumbling. But there are worse people than the grumblers. There are those who are always disputing. I don't think that Christians are always expected to agree with each other, but I do think we are expected to disagree agreeably, and never to break fellowship. And there were two ladies in the church at Philippi who were in danger of doing this very thing, Euodia and Syntyche. Paul speaks to them about this and beseeches them to agree in the Lord, for they had 'Laboured side by side' with him in the Gospel. They were not on the periphery of the Church, they were right in the very heart of it. Paul knew the sort of thing that would happen. People would notice their long faces, and begin to take sides in the disagreement, and then, from the best of motives, the fellowship would be broken. If you are living in the light of the fact that Jesus is coming back you can't afford divisions in the fellowship. If you're not shining in the church because there is division about all sorts of little things, your light will never shine outside the church either.

Jesus once said, 'I am the Light of the world.' And he said to his disciples 'You are the lights of the world.' Here Paul says 'Among whom you shine as lights of the world.' That doesn't make sense. How can Jesus, the disciples, you and I be the lights of the world? Two or three years ago I went to see my daughter who's a missionary in Central Africa. One evening we went out for a walk. It was a lovely night with a beautiful full moon. The stars shining and there was not a cloud in the sky. As we walked on that jungle path, she said to me, 'Isn't the moon shining brightly,' and I agreed that

Living in the Light of His Return

it was lovely. Then I said to her, 'How stupid can we be. The moon doesn't shine. The moon can't shine, it's only a lump of material that has no capacity to shine – our astronauts have confirmed that. But it's in orbit in relation to the sun, and when it turns its face heavenward and sunward, it catches the glow and reflects that light into the darkness of our world. That makes me really excited, because it is exactly what a Christian does. You can't shine, and I can't shine, but we can turn our eyes upon Jesus and look full on his wonderful face and catch the glow and warmth there, and reflect him into the darkness of the world.

Do everything without murmuring, without disputing, keep your lights blazing brightly so that the world may see the love, the warmth, the reality of Christ in your life every day. Christians living in the light of Jesus' return have no room for division in their fellowship, and if there is division, it must be brought to the cross.

'Our commonwealth is in heaven and from it we await a Saviour, the Lord Jesus Christ who will change our lowly body to be like his glorious body by the power which enables him even to subject all things to himself' (Phil. 3:20, 21.) Two words there need clarification. The A.V. rendering is 'Our conversation is in heaven.' Usually in the Bible that refers to our manner of life, but here it means 'Citizenship' or 'State to which I belong'. For this world isn't where we belong. Our citizenship is somewhere else, for Christians belong to glory. Again the A.V. reads 'From when we look for the Saviour.' That word 'Look' is a very weak word. The Greek it translates means 'Eager expectation'. Because we eagerly await his coming there will be a striking contrast in comparison with all other people. Paul implies in this letter that there were people whose manner of life was undermining the effectiveness of the gospel at Philippi. So for their edification, Paul exhorts all Christians to observe how he himself lived. I don't think many of us would be prepared to say, 'I beseech you brethren, join in imitating me and mark those who so live as you have an example in us.' It is interesting that this word 'Example' is the same in the Greek as that used in John chapter twenty verse twenty-five to mean 'Print of the nails'. So what Paul is in effect saying is that the mark of the nails, of Calvary, is on his life and should be on theirs (marking it out from unbelievers' lives) as reality all the way through. The enemies of the church at Philippi were not heathens, nor Jews, but andemonians, connected with the Church but interpreting Christian liberty as freedom from all moral restraint. They were preaching and living a false gospel in which the reality of the cross had no part, the marks of the nails were not on them. A Christian living in the light of the fact that Jesus is coming soon has no room for sin in his life, because on his life God has put the marks of Calvary.

A Christian living in the light of Jesus' return has no room for sin in his life because he is part of the colony of heaven. Here is what the day of Christ should be doing for us when the truth begins to grip us. No room for idols in my heart, no room for slackness in my service, no room for division in my fellowship, no room for sin in my life. You may be inclined to say, 'Absolutely impossible'. But from God's point of view it is not only possible but totally logical, because every demand he makes upon my life is met by the power of the Holy Spirit in me. Have you got that principle of holy living, living in the light of Jesus' return – every

Living in the Light of His Return

demand that a holy God can make upon you any time is met by the life he has put into your heart?

So I leave you with that tremendous promise in this fourth chapter. 'My God shall supply all your needs according to his riches in glory by Christ Jesus' (v. 19). Did you know that God has at least four accounts? – 'The riches of his goodness' (Romans 2:4); 'The riches of his wisdom' (Romans 11:13); 'The riches of his grace' (Eph. 1:7); 'The riches of his glory' (Eph. 1:18). So we can be sure that when we answer the call to live in the light of Jesus' return, he has abundant supply to meet our every need right up until that wonderful day.

STRENGTH OF WEAKNESS AND WEAKNESS OF STRENGTH
(2 Corinthians 12:9, 10)

by the Revd. Dr. Alan Redpath

You may think the title rather unusual. If you think into it most of us make these discoveries in the reverse order. Our eyes are opened to see how hopelessly weak our imagined strength is, and find the answer in discovering that when we are weak then we are strong only in the power of the risen Saviour (2 Cor. 12:9–10).

There was a man who imagined himself to be strong, and eventually came to know his utter weakness. In his case, alas, he was too late to do anything about it. The vision of youth came to Solomon when he was in his teens. His father died and a scramble for the throne resulted. However, Solomon became the choice of the people as he was the choice of his father and the choice of God. Out of the line of the true succession, because he was the product of a tragedy in David's life. Immediately he acceded to the throne, God spoke to him in a dream. 'Ask what I shall give you' (1 Kings 3:5). This is how God always speaks to us. 'Ask and it will be given to you; seek, and you will find; knock and it will be opened to you' (Matt. 7:7). This is a blank cheque on

Strength of Weakness and Weakness of Strength

the 'Bank of Heaven' freely offered by the Lord Jesus Christ. What was Solomon's answer? He did not want a request at all. At least not to begin with. He reminded the Lord (v. 6) of the kind of father he had, and that he owed all he was to the mercy of God. David had been a great man, but Solomon saw that the reason for his greatness was something much more than personal qualities of life. What insight Solomon had to the principle that it is gentleness which makes a man great. 'I am but a little child . . . ' says Solomon. I do not think he was ever quite as great again as when he admitted his dependence upon God for everything. That is the only way to begin with him, and the only way to go with him. 'Except you are converted and become as little children, you shall not see the kingdom of God,' said Jesus.

See, too, what Solomon told the Lord he needed. 'Thy servant is in the midst of thy people . . . Give me therefore an understanding mind . . . that I may discern between good and evil' (vv. 8–9). He was about to endure all the pressure of other people's lives, and surely the whole issue in the daily experience of us all is just there; how we come through trial and triumph, in contact with others. So Solomon had only one thing to ask, a heart that understands how to discern between good and bad. As a youngster God had told him what were his right priorities. He knew the strength of weakness.

Solomon became a master organiser, a great financier. He had forty thousand stalls of horses and twelve thousand horsemen. He spoke three thousand proverbs, and wrote over one thousand songs (1 Kings 4:26, 32). The greatest people from the civilised world visited him, and were staggered by his wisdom. None more so than the Queen of Sheba (1 Kings 10:1). It was not his riches which attracted the Arabian queen, but his fame concerning the name of the Lord. Her visit revealed to her what the government of God really means: 'Blessed be the Lord your God, who has delighted in you and set you on the throne of Israel! Because the Lord loved Israel for ever, he has made you king, that you may execute justice and righteousness' (10:9). She saw in him exactly what he had seen in his own father, namely that the secret of everything lies in the sovereignty of the living Lord.

Solomon's greatest achievement was the building of the temple. It arose without a sound (1 Kings 6:7), more magnificent than any other. Yet even it was useless without the presence of God, and therefore the king sent for the Ark (8:6). The whole nation was present at the sacrifice, and the glory of God filled the house. What a reminder this was of his dealing in earlier days with Moses and Aaron. 'They went into the tent of meeting; and when they came out they blessed the people, and the glory of the Lord appeared to all the people. And the fire . . . consumed the offering.' (Leviticus 9:23). This unique sign of divine approval is only the result of obedience on the part of those who are strengthened, enlightened and quieted. There is no short cut to mature spiritual strength, which is the outcome of waiting upon God until human weakness is endued with his mighty power.

Solomon knew this, and his prayer at the dedication of the temple is probably without equal in the word of God. He commenced his prayer standing, with his hands raised and ended it on his knees, still with his hands raised. This man felt the grip of eternity, and surely at this point he rose to great heights. Here is the real crisis, the most critical time in life. God seeks to come to

Strength of Weakness and Weakness of Strength

terms with Solomon (chapter 9). Either live faithfully under my orders, in which case my blessing will be with you, or else go your own way and bring your country to ruin. The terms are just the same today. It is a critical moment for the Lord to appear to Solomon. The accomplishment of a work is a dangerous time when the temptation is to take the credit for it, and then to relax and take it easy. Solomon tragically failed. He had not yet learned the weakness of strength. The dangers of success, to the false valour of considering maturity the end product, and therefore resting on the oars of our own human achievement.

In his later years, Solomon's wisdom went on parade. Kings and queens from afar came to hear him (10:24). Now he had both wisdom and wealth, and his feet slipped with the combined push of both. Every cup Solomon had was gold. He amassed millions in a year, until it submerged him. Even in accomplishing his greatest vision, the temple, he betrayed a breakdown in character. It took him only seven years to build it, but it took him nearly twice that time to build his own home. However strong our zeal for the Lord may be, if the time devoted to our own ease and comfort is greater than that we give to him, we are only proving that the master passion of our lives is selfish rather than godly. Yet it was Solomon himself who wrote 'Pride comes before destruction' (Proverbs 16:18). It was he who looked back on the whole of his life and exclaimed, 'Vanity of vanities! All is vanity.' (Eccles. 1:2.) However, that was all secondary. From childhood there had been a fatal chink in his armour. Was the reason for it in David's licentiousness? Had it sprung from that illicit affair with Bathsheba? But Solomon allowed that fatal weakness to develop. The first step to disaster was taken at the very beginning, when he married the king of Egypt's daughter (3:1). He was wise enough to know better, but for all his wisdom he was stirring up trouble for the future in becoming unequally yoked with an unbeliever. Wise, yes; obedient, no. And the result was bound to follow in the absence of repentence.

There is another 'but' about Solomon. 'But Solomon loved many foreign women' (11:1). He had allowed Satan to get through a weak spot and then fan out over other areas of life with the result that Solomon's fellowship with his Lord lay in ruins (11:4). Spiritual reality gone, deep spiritual experience a thing of the past, and disaster struck. It is almost unbelievable that a man who had so walked with God had come to a point where God had to speak to him in anger (11:9-11).

What a tragic statement! The man who built the temple, presided over its dedication, cried to God for his abiding presence, now turned from his loyalty, broke his covenant and all in response to a sensual nature. God's anger was not passive. He raised up three adversaries against Solomon. The promise of a long life was never fulfilled, because he had refused the conditions and he died in his early sixties. No man can step outside the government of God. The warmth of the fire which blesses is God's action. I can plan my way in regard to the fire, but the steps I take are governed by God. What has God to say to us about all this? The greatest temptations which will ever attack us in life are those that attacked Solomon – money and sex. Let in the devil in these areas and he will percolate your very being and ruin your walk with God.

Repentence followed by obedience. A determination to forsake that which threatens the Lord's mastery in your life – these are the lessons we must learn. 'We must

Strength of Weakness and Weakness of Strength

obey God' was the rallying cry of the New Testament church. 'God has given his Holy Spirit to them that obey him,' was his answer, and that can be true in your life. To quote Charles Finney, 'Revival . . . is nothing less than a new beginning of obedience to God; a breaking of heart and getting down into the dust before him, with deep humility and forsaking of sin. A revival breaks the power of the world and of sin over Christians. The charm of the world is broken, and the power of sin is overcome. Truths to which our hearts are unresponsive suddenly become living. Whereas mind and conscience may assent to truth, when revival comes, obedience to the truth is the one thing that matters.'

THE WAY OF RENEWAL

by the Revd. Dr. Alan Redpath

I find it very exciting to be alive these days because against the background of anarchy and revolution, the Lord is doing a new thing. And we are seeing renewal and revival in many different countries. Many more people are becoming convinced that Jesus Christ is not only relevant, he is the vital factor. With this in mind I want to look at Romans chapter eight which is a tremendous description of the Christian battlefield. Out from this word of God there stand three basic principles concerning Christian living; what it really means. *How the power gets through. How it is maintained. And how it is all possible in your life now.* Some defeated, lonely, depressed, sad, dejected Christian may have his life absolutely transformed by the power of the Spirit of God.

The first thing in this chapter is that when the Holy Spirit comes into my life he imparts a new nature. As verse four states, this is so that the just requirement of the law might be fulfilled in us by the Spirit. The righteousness of God's law fulfilled all the demands met

The Way of Renewal

by the Spirit of God residing and occupying our hearts. Peter said, 'You remember you are partakers of the divine nature.' How often in his letters Paul would say, 'Put off the old nature, put on the new.' A constant battle all the time between the flesh and the Spirit. You receive this new nature when you are born again. That is, when you come to Jesus absolutely broken, helpless, destitute, knowing that you just haven't got what it takes to live, and you feel that life is absolutely hopeless, and you are helpless to do a thing about it. That is the point where God meets with you. And at that point in answer to your repentance and your trust in the crucified risen Lord he imparts to you his Holy Spirit. He comes at that moment. 'If any man has not the Spirit of Christ he is none of his' (v. 9). We are all baptised by one Spirit into one body, and we have all been made to drink of one Spirit. At that moment a new dimension of life has begun and Jesus by his Spirit lives within us, and his life cannot possibly sin. He is God, therefore he cannot sin and he becomes the instrument in your life for victory.

My second proposition from this chapter will present some problems to you. The nature with which I was born, the old nature, continues to exist in the regenerate heart. So as a Christian I have within me a new life that cannot sin. But I have also an old nature that can do nothing but sin. Constantly the downward bias is to sin and to failure, and I keep right to the very end of the journey what this book calls *the flesh*.

In this great victory chapter of the Bible we have twelve references to the flesh and twelve references to the Spirit in constant battle every day. What is the flesh? What do you think the word means? It's not this fourteen stone or thereabouts of matter I carry around with me. The answer is *self*. In my heart there is the 'Jesus-life' that can never sin, and there is a 'self-life' that can never do anything else but sin. There is my battle. Some people would tell us that when you become a Christian this *self* is completely erradicated. If that were true Romans chapter eight wouldn't be in my Bible. However, alongside a sinful nature that could do nothing but fail there is the nature of God who cannot possibly fail. These two are alongside one another, and *self* is all that I am apart from Jesus. The Living Bible vividly describes what *self* really is, and I like this rendering: 'I know I am rotten through and through so far as my old sinful nature is concerned. No matter which way I turn I can't make myself do right. I want to but I can't. When I want to do good, I don't, and when I try not to do wrong, I do it anyway. Now if I am doing what I don't want to, it is plain where the trouble is: sin still has me in its evil grasp. It seems to be a fact of life that when I want to do what is right, I inevitably do what is wrong. I love to do God's will as far as my new nature is concerned; but there is something else deep within me, in my lower nature, that is at war with my mind and wins the fight and makes me a slave to the sin that is still within me. In my mind I want to be God's willing servant but instead I find myself enslaved to sin. So you see how it is: my new life tells me to do right, but the old nature that is still inside me loves to sin. Oh, what a terrible predicament I'm in! Who will free me from my slavery to this deadly lower nature? Thank God! It has been done by Jesus Christ our Lord. He has set me free' (Romans 7:18).

What a tremendous passage that is, do you get the thrust of it? The new nature is Jesus, Jesus in us by his Holy Spirit. The old nature is myself and all I am,

The Way of Renewal

apart from him. Paul says that *self* is sold to sin and it can do nothing but sin. God never tries to make it better. His strategy is to replace you with Jesus so that Jesus might come in and live his life in you day by day by the Spirit. 'Those who live according to the flesh set their minds on the things of the flesh, but those who live according to the Spirit set their minds on the things of the Spirit so then brethren we are debtors not to the flesh to live according to the flesh for if you live according to the flesh you will die, but if by the spirit you put to death the deeds of the flesh you will live.' There you have it. There's the sharp distinction. The choice between life and death. It doesn't matter what your profession of faith may be. If you are constantly living after the flesh you'll die says Paul. If the Holy Spirit has come in and taken control, and lifted you above the flesh you live. C. H. Spurgeon said that an unholy life is the evidence of an unchanged heart and an unchanged heart is the evidence of an unsaved soul. The call of the New Testament is to holy living, the call of God in these days of his people is to holy living. But the Holy Spirit within me, within you, has power to overcome that old nature. The law of the Spirit of life, says verse two, has set me free from the law of sin and death. The Holy Spirit only fulfils in me what Jesus Christ did for me on the Cross. And so in the Holy Spirit I have the one who has power to overcome the old nature. But the power of God's spirit takes possession and the working of his power is dependent entirely upon the extent of my submission to him. If I submit he goes on delivering, but if I stop yielding he stops working. He has power to deliver and I must learn what it is, day by day, to yield to that power.

This is the victory: the law of the Spirit of life in

Christ hath set me free from the law of sin and death. The downward drag of the old nature is there, but when I turn in faith to Jesus, that is replaced by another law that comes in and lifts me up, the law of the Spirit in Christ and enables me to ride above the situation and to triumph in Jesus. But I've got to yield to that law. We all think we can do it ourselves, but once we begin to fight for victory we're heading for defeat. I often pray, 'Lord save me from the tensions of trying to get my own victories.' My part in this life of victory in Jesus is just this. First, I must yield my life unconditionally to him. If anyone is looking for Holy Spirit experience but is not prepared to submit to Holy Spirit control, that's just sham. You must learn to submit to Holy Spirit control every day of your life, put yourself under that new law and the Holy Spirit will lift you up. What will be the result of that transaction? The result of it will be just this, that for the first time in your life the fruit of the Spirit will get through you. The Holy Spirit will be let loose in your heart, the Lord Jesus Himself will live his life through you and other people will begin to sense reality, love, life and power.

We are engaged, these days, in tremendous spiritual warfare. On the one hand a supernatural force of evil has got this world in control and seeking to bring it to disaster. Perhaps you don't believe in the devil, well all I can say is that is being very unkind to humanity. If you really imagine that all the filth, rottenness, sin and evil that goes on today in the world is accountable simply by human people, without being inspired by satanic force, that is beyond me. But on the other hand there's a great supernatural power of righteousness alive, lifting lives out of the dung hill, transforming them, making them pure, making them like Jesus – that's the battle. Whose

The Way of Renewal

side are you on? There is no neutral ground. I wonder if you are on Jesus' side? But if you take the step of faith, in the power of the Spirit, trust him to reveal the fruit of the Spirit in your heart, let Jesus loose in your life and come under his control, you will know his freedom. There is power in the Holy Spirit to overcome the old nature. But you must claim in order that you might experience by faith that power right now.

FREEDOM OF THE SPIRIT
(Ephesians 5:18, 19)

by the Revd. Canon Harry Sutton

It was once said that the Holy Spirit is the lost dynamic of the Church. Some people believe that the hard times on which the Church in the United Kingdom has fallen are due largely to the fact that we have been over-occupied with methods, techniques, and liturgies almost to the neglect of the person and work of God the Holy Spirit in our midst. However, today it can be claimed that the Holy Spirit is no longer the neglected person in the trinity, for we live in an age for which there has been all over the world a re-discovery of God the Holy Spirit in the life of the individual believer and in the corporate life of the Church.

Many of us are disturbed by the weakness and apparent impotence of the Church, and of our own personal failures in living an effective Christian life. We are thankful for what God has done in us and for what the Lord is doing for us, but for so many of us there is a longing for something better in our Christian experience. In fact, I would regard this as one of the encouraging features of Church life today that almost wherever

Freedom of The Spirit

I go I find ministers and lay people who are increasingly aware of a need for something fuller and richer in their own Christian experience. But why is it that so many of us, while possessing the Spirit are not filled by the Spirit? Charles Finney once wrote, 'Christians are as guilty for not being filled with the Spirit as sinners for not repenting. They are the more so as they have more light and so they are more guilty.' I fear that far too many of us go through life without ever realising our full potential for God. A Roman Catholic Cardinal on the Continent recently said, 'I believe in the surprises of the Holy Spirit and far too many of us have ceased to expect the unexpected to happen in our lives.' My hope is that an increasing number of Christian people in this country, while not seeking that which is sensational or spectacular will nevertheless daily expect the unexpected to happen in their lives.

I think the day has come when in our churches and in our individual life we've got to expect the unusual to happen in our midst, for I believe the Church of which we are members is an unusual Church, it's a supernatural body of people. We are not just a bag of bones, we are the body of Christ on earth. And so many of us are longing for the surprises of the Holy Spirit. Not a temporary spiritual pick-me-up but something that represents the pulse-beat of our lives. A normal relaxed flowing fullness in the Holy Spirit that represents a poise and balance of Christian living that glorifies God in the world. Most of us can say that we are experiencing every day the grace of God, but how many of us can say that we are experiencing the *abundant* grace of God, spoken of in John's gospel (1:16). Many of us can say that we have joy deep down in our hearts since Jesus came in and that's good, but only a few of us, I fear, can say we have abundant joy in our hearts, the kind of abundant joy referred to in Corinthians (2 Cor. 8:2). Most experience a measure of very real Christian peace in our hearts, but how many of us can truly claim that we have abundance of peace referred to in Jeremiah (33:6). All these passages, I believe, and many others indicate that the Christian life is meant to be something extraordinary. I do not mean that we should be looking for that which is exciting, sensational and dramatic but rather for abundant, liberating, relaxing and uninhibiting life in the Spirit. That is what the Bible teaches and that this is God's norm for us.

Some may say, 'That's all very well but we genuinely do try to witness for Christ in our corner of the vineyard and so few people seem to be interested that sometimes we are tempted to ask "Will we ever see the Holy Spirit at work in our lives?".' Not long ago a very close friend of mine whom I love very much indeed and whom I respect very highly, a clergyman, and I were having fellowship together in prayer, and after we had been praying a moment or two I was aware of the fact that he was crying. When I asked him what had upset him, he answered, 'You were speaking tonight of the urgent need for Christians to win other people for Christ, and that those of us who are clergymen should pray that we might be released from professionalism in order to win people for the Lord Jesus.' He said, 'I'm crying because I don't remember when I last led a soul to Christ.' That clergyman speaks for very many Christian people today in the United Kingdom. He has prayed hard and he has worked hard. And yet at the end of the day there is not a lot to see for it.

What is the way forward in all this? Is there an answer or do we have to struggle all the days of our

Freedom of The Spirit

life? I believe that the Christian should not live an 'up and down' spiritual life. The fullness of the Holy Spirit is intended to be the continual state of the Christian. Why then are so many of us not enjoying this fullness? Basically it is a problem of the will. There are no short cuts. The fullness of the Spirit is dependent upon an act of the will, focusing faith and bringing Christian discipline to bear. If we choose that kind of life then we also choose fullness of the Spirit. We may choose, if we wish, to sacrifice that kind of a life for a feeble impotent experience. Why do we sometimes choose weakness rather than strength? For many Christians the answer is that they disregard the presence of the Holy Spirit in their lives. 'Know ye not that ye are the temple of God and that the Spirit of God dwelleth in you.' Some Christians live as though they had no heavenly guest residing within them and they never regard the presence of the Holy Spirit as being within them. I deliberately recall every morning on waking the truth that in my being I am the tabernacle, or the tent, or the temple of God the Holy Spirit. We must acknowledge daily the holy presence that dwells within us, for the truth is that we are honoured and privileged to be the temples of the Holy Spirit. So the first thing I would say is that weakness in the Christian is often traced to a disregard of the presence of the Holy Spirit in the life of the believer.

Secondly, weakness follows because we disobey the promptings of the Holy Spirit. When he seeks to correct us we sidestep the issue. Because we can so easily hide from others we think we can as easily hide from God. So when the Spirit prompts, convicts, somehow or another we hide from him. Very rarely, if ever, do we allow ourselves to be brought to the point of genuine repentance and sorrow for the thing about which the Spirit is prompting us. To be obedient to the promptings of the Holy Spirit is one of the most urgent needs of our day. It was Martin Luther who said, 'I would rather obey than work miracles.' And obedience is the way, I believe, to success in the Christian life. In the Acts of the Apostles, demonstrations of spiritual power were almost invariably preceded by periods of repentance by believers who felt that they had disobeyed the promptings of the Spirit. I am at the moment doing some study into the history of revival over the last one hundred years, and especially in the United Kingdom. I have not yet come across a single instance of revival that has not been preceded by a period of repentance by individual Christians and by the corporate life of the Church. Not a single instance. Although I believe that in the end revival is part of the sovereign act of God, that the initiative in revival is with him, I'm also coming to the understanding that God very rarely acts totally apart from man, and that the thing he expects to see in us as the forerunner of revival is obedience to the promptings of God the Holy Spirit demonstrating itself in repentance before the Lord.

Thirdly, I see the path of weakness as a path along which we distrust his leading. Paul could boast, 'I was not disobedient to the heavenly vision.' Now it's not always easy to understand the leading of the Spirit. For instance, the call of Philip to leave a thriving revival in Samaria where he was a key man to go to a desert strip called Gaza was one of the most unusual calls that any man ever had. As far as common sense was concerned it made nonsense. Yet in obedience to the leading of God Philip went to the desert. And in the desert a miracle takes place. He met, not just an ordin-

Freedom of The Spirit

ary Ethiopian, but the man who was the chancellor of the exchequer of Ethiopia, and meeting him led him into the wonderful and fantastic blessing. I don't know the full consequences of that blessing, but I'm sure they must have been enormous. So while on the human level the leading seemed to make nonsense, yet in the economy and will of God it was full of sense. And there was no questioning about this leading of the Spirit. When led by the Spirit we must resist the temptation to ask why, when, or where. Frequently we dig up in unbelief what we have sown in faith. Let us lay aside distrust. Let us be implicitly obedient to the leading of the Spirit and we shall discover that in such leading we will find the power of God at our disposal waiting to call us into a new kind of fullness that will glorify his name in the world.

So I see our weakness, among other things, as a tendency to disregard the presence of the Holy Spirit in our lives. We disobey his promptings all too often and we tend to distrust his leading. If then, these are some of the reasons why we do not enjoy the fullness of the Spirit, how do we come to know this fullness and enjoy it? Happily, the New Testament is full and clear on this teaching. There are two key words to the fullness of the Spirit. 1. Repentance. 2. Obedience. Without those two experiences the fullness of the Spirit cannot really be enjoyed by the believer. When these two are realities in our lives then we may confidently expect a liberation of the Spirit. 'The law of the spirit of life in Christ Jesus hath made me free from the law of sin and death' (Romans 8:2).

Deliverance from the power of indwelling sin is God's will for everyone of us. Before conversion we were subject to the law of sin and death; after it, by virtue of our union with Christ and the indwelling of the Spirit, we are subject to a new law, the law of the spirit of life. This new law is stronger than the old law, setting us free from the power of sin, releasing us to be free in the service of our Lord and Saviour Jesus Christ. I find this liberating influence of the Holy Spirit wholly meaningful in my experience today. For instance, it liberates me intellectually. When I say the Spirit has illuminated my intellect I don't want you to get a wrong impression. What I mean is that as a result of being liberated by the Spirit, I now think at levels at which I could never think before. My intellectual horizons have been made much larger, fuller, so that I can more easily perceive the things of God, so that I am sensitive to sin, so that I recognise the devil, so that I can see God in all his glory and all his beauty. My intellect has been enriched and liberated by the Spirit. And so to a greater or lesser degree have my emotions and my moral life. There is such a thing as false freedom, freedom to do what you like. And there's such a thing as true freedom, and that's freedom to do what you ought. It's always more difficult to do what you ought than to do what you like, and freedom in the Spirit gives a man the power to do what he ought to do, come what may. A very close friend of mine used to work in the city of London but he felt that the line of business he was in was inconsistent with all his beliefs. He came to the point where he had to do what he ought to do, and it cost him £9,000 a year. I said to him, 'Well, having done what you ought to do, are you sorry?' 'No,' he said, 'as a matter of fact, I have found it a wholly enriching experience.' Free to do what we ought to do, that's what I'm speaking of when I talk about a liberation of emotions and of morals. It's a very practical liberation. It's something

Freedom of The Spirit

that works in the nitty gritty situations of everyday life; my relationship to my wife, my children, my friends, to any department of life is wholly enriched by this liberating experience of the Holy Spirit.

Secondly, where there is repentance and obedience there is also life in the Spirit. Life in the Spirit, as I understand and experience it, is both qualitative and contagious. By qualitative I mean that 'The chief evidence of fullness of the Holy Spirit is moral evidence and not miraculous,' to quote John Stott. Being filled with the Spirit brings a quality, creates a dimension, unknown without the Spirit because our life of the flesh cannot bring this about. This quality is seen in terms of the fruit of the Spirit.

I find this very interesting because it's at this point that very many Christians have some difficulties. This quality of life that we call the fruit of the Spirit referred (Galatians 5), is a quality that we have to display in its totality. The gifts of the Spirit are rather different. The Holy Spirit scatters his gifts among the congregation. It is part of the responsibility of the local congregation to discover its spiritual resources, asking 'Which gifts do we have among us,' so that they can be used to the glory of God. When we come to the fruit of the Spirit this is not so. The fruit is not scattered among the congregation so that one person has love, another person has peace and another person faith. What the New Testament teaches at this point is that all nine facets that we call the fruit of the Spirit must be displayed in and by the believer. And the measure in which the fruit is borne in us is precisely the measure in which we are filled with the Spirit. Fullness of the Spirit will bear fullness of fruit. A dearth of the Spirit will bring forth a dearth of the fruit. And so it is, that there is a quality about the way in which the life of the Spirit is demonstrated. Having said that I would be false to what I am finding to be true and to my understanding of the Bible if I said that the supernatural, therefore, plays no part in this life in the Spirit. I agree that the moral aspect should come first but don't think that we should put a full-stop there, because I believe that the Holy Spirit is working through people in wonderful ways that can only be described as miraculous. And I am finding wherever I go around the world that life in the Spirit, while in the first place consisting of a moral quality, ought not to be totally divested of the miraculous dimension. So life in the Spirit is qualitative in the first place in a moral way, and in the second place in a demonstrative way.

I also believe that life in the Spirit is not only qualitative but that it is contagious. People often ask me what I think accounts for the growth of the Pentecostal church in Latin America which is the fastest growing church in the world. Together with the other evangelical churches in Latin America it's growing at a rate of ten per cent per annum, three times faster than the birthrate growth in Latin America which is the highest in the world. The reason for this growth, I believe, is that this church has the contagious aspect of life in the Spirit. It's qualitative and it's contagious. By that I mean they are motivated and trained to win others for Christ and this is as a result of their knowing the Holy Spirit as they do. My hope for the Church in the United Kingdom is that there will be a contagious dimension about our Christian witness. That we'll want to share the love of Jesus with others in a relaxed way wherever we go.

In conclusion, I believe that where there is repentance

Freedom of The Spirit

and obedience, this will not only lead to liberation by the Spirit and life in the Spirit but that there will be a clear leading of the Spirit. The fullness of the Spirit leads to a Spirit-led life. This is emphatically true for every one of us. Let us look to Jesus to see what we ought to be, and then we can look to the Holy Spirit and ask him to make us what we ought to be. The believer today lives in a very complex age and the situation in which we live may well call for new ideas, new patterns of ministry, new experimental forms of worship, but above all else the age calls for men and women who are filled with the Spirit. The Holy Spirit is willing and desirous to do this for us in the wholeness of his work. We cannot be filled with the Spirit until we are prepared to yield ourselves to be led by the Spirit and by the power of his might. The great hindrance in most of our lives is the self-life and the world. God wants to bestow his fullness upon us. Our faith may expect it with the greatest possible confidence, the one thing that is essential is true repentance, faithful obedience and a continual day-by-day living faith in the Lord Jesus. Where that is so the living water will surely flow from within us and out to a parched and thirsty world.

SERVANTS OF THE KING
(2 Corinthians 4:5)

by the Revd. Canon Harry Sutton

A great deal has been lost I think in our evangelical thinking and our Christian experience by treating the initial things of the Christian faith as the final things. What I mean by that is this, that although it is all-important that we should come to know the Lord Jesus Christ as our Saviour and everlasting friend, there are other truths to be learned. Though we are born as babes in Christ we possess the potential for Christian growth. That potential, of course, is to be found in the working of God the Holy Spirit within us. However, one of the problems that face us today is that too many become absorbed in the initial things, and too few give the same kind of thought and discipline of heart and of mind to the concept of growing in the Christian life. This means that many live in a kind of eternal childhood so that pastors become nothing more than baby-sitters. They spend nine-tenths of their ministry watching the babies.

In first Thessalonians chapter five Jesus is simply called 'the Lord', and that means something more than mere human authority. It is the New Testament equivalent of the Old Testament title 'Jehovah'. It refers to the divinity of the Lord. It speaks of authority, both human and divine. And it is a significant one for the believer. It was one that was well known in our Lord's own day. Lord was the name that the slave called his master. Lord was a word that the Romans used by way of a greeting. They greeted each other with a phrase like 'Caesar is lord'. And the reply, 'He is lord indeed.' So when Christians came along and said 'Jesus is Lord' this was revolutionary indeed. This was saying, there was a greater authority than Caesar. It is the Lord Jesus Christ. Jesus is Lord. Throughout the Bible we have this concept of the kingdom and the King, with Jesus being the supreme ruler. He is the Lord of every department of life, and makes far-reaching demands on every one of us. So often in our Christian experience we pick and choose over which area of our lives Jesus will have control. For instance, I imagine it's fair to say that in very few instances the Lord Jesus Christ would be Lord of the cellar of our lives. He would be Lord of some of the other rooms. But when it comes down to the cellar, the innermost being of us, the dark spots, only in rare cases does one detect that Jesus is Lord of the cellar. However, we may not pick and choose. If he is going to be Lord at all, then he must be Lord of all. And this relationship between the believer and the Lord Jesus is vital if he is to make a success of the Christian life. The question then arises, in what way should we show our devotion and submit to the lordship of the Lord Jesus Christ? I want to suggest three ways in which I, personally, am trying to come to grips in my own experience with the lordship of Christ.

First of all, I suggest that as loyal subjects of the King

we should have a concern for the King's glory in the world. When I have the joy of leading a soul to Christ I am always glad for that person's sake. I am glad, that they have been passed from death to life, from darkness to light, from error to truth. But I am even more glad that in the salvation of that soul the Lord Jesus Christ has been glorified. And so it is that in winning others we glorify the King. In Acts chapter eleven, we read that the granting of repentance unto life to the Gentiles brought glory to God. We glorify the King by winning others for the Lord Jesus. And as evangelical Christians we should learn the difference between reaching others for Christ, and winning others for Christ. We can spend all our time reaching others for Christ and we may be successful in doing so. We could, in fact, reach the whole of Great Britain for the Lord Jesus Christ by tomorrow without necessarily winning a single person for Christ. What I am suggesting brings glory to the Lord Jesus Christ is when we actually win others for the Lord Jesus Christ. How else does the Church grow. If those who do know are failing to tell those who do not know, then we must not be surprised if the Church does not grow.

We may show our concern for the King's glory in the world in other ways, also by serving others for Christ. Feeding the hungry, clothing the naked, healing the sick, are all praiseworthy ends in themselves. But when, as I often do, I see someone come into one of our Mission stations in the last stages of an illness and after a period of skilled nursing they walk out healthy, I am glad for the person who came. I could hardly be more delighted for the people in Northern Argentina who fifteen or sixteen years ago would die because there was no one to heal them, but who today, through the min-

Servants of the King

istry of Christ's Church no longer die prematurely but live. I am glad for them. But I am more delighted that in this health and strength and new found prosperity Jesus is glorified through this ministry. We glorify the King on earth in our endeavours to win others for Christ and in our sharing of our substance with others so that they may live a balanced healthy life. So when we subscribe to TEAR Fund and similar agencies it is not just a show of benevolence. It is supremely more. In those things we are glorifying the Son on the earth.

There is a second way, I believe, in which we bring glory to the King and that is by fruit-bearing. 'Herein is my Father glorified,' said Jesus, 'that ye bear much fruit, so shall you be my disciples' (John 15). If the Father is glorified then I believe the Son and the Holy Spirit is glorified at the same time. So, Jesus is glorified by our fruit-bearing. I see fruit-bearing as relating to Galatians chapter five. Quite clearly it must relate to that, but I also see it relating to another kind of fruit-bearing. The fruit-bearing that I have already referred to and which I must now underline. The fruit-bearing that demonstrates itself in winning others for Christ. It is in our fruit-bearing that the Lord Jesus is glorified in the world.

There is a third way in which we may honour the King, and it is that we should be obedient to the King's commands. Let us just look at two of these commands. Jesus said, 'Follow me.' It is interesting to note that when our Lord said that to the fishermen, they did not ask on what terms do you want us to follow you or, where do you want us to go. When Jesus said follow me, they left their father, their boats, and nets and they followed him. It is quite true that at a later date they returned to their nets and to their boats, but in some instances when we begin to follow Jesus there is no return. For instance Matthew. When he heard the call, 'Come, follow,' there was no return for him because he was a collector of taxes and as he collected the taxes he would be regarded as a traitor to the Jews. However, when he left the tax table and followed Jesus, he would be regarded as a traitor to the Romans. So there was no return for Matthew. So much of our following today has safety nets. We follow but we have also prepared for the day when maybe we do not. But that is not the kind of following that is going to show loyal allegiance to the King. It is interesting to note that invariably when God calls us to follow it is accompanied by a promise. For instance when the Lord called Abraham, 'Get thee out hence', there was also the promise 'And I will make of thee a great nation.' Take up the cross, follow me, were commands from Jesus accompanied by the promise, 'Thou shalt have treasure in heaven.' The command to follow may not always say where we are to follow, but invariably the command is accompanied by a precious promise.

Here is another command that I am finding challenging in my own experience. Love one another. As I look back over my Christian experience, my opinion is (and this I say with utmost sensitivity and respect) that most evangelical Christians are long on faith but short on love. For years, my main concern has been faith, and I do not regret that, but I wish that over the years I had been as long on love as I have been on faith. It does seem to me that in this area some of us are at our weakest. And you will recall that the kind of love that we are to display to each other, and indeed to the world, is a love which if needs be calls us to die in the interests of others. The New Testament makes it clear that love

Servants of the King

will outlast all other gifts. They will fade away but love will last. And if we are meant to love each other then it must be right for us to look each other in the eye occasionally and say so. Let us say from time to time, 'I love you.'

Finally, our third demonstration of loyalty to the King must be that we should prepare for the King's return. There are many different views about how the Lord Jesus Christ will come, that there's a sort of unofficial truce among preachers that you don't say anything at all. Well I'm going to say something. People say to me, are you an a-millenialist, a pre-millenialist or a post-millenialist. No, I reply, I am a pan-millenialist. They say, a pan-millenialist? Yes, I say, I believe that everything will pan out all right in the end. Christian friends, he's coming back. Praise the Lord! And if that is so let us prepare for his coming back. How do we prepare? It is not easy, but it is right. And the right thing for us to do is to prepare for his coming by taking part in God's plan for the world before he comes. The order of events is this: God's programme is first the evangelisation of the world, then the coming of the King (Mark 13:10 and Matthew 24:14). So, whatever may be our differences about the rapture and the millenium, there can be no difference in the belief, it seems to me, that before the Lord comes the world must be evangelised. That everyone must hear and understand the consequences of accepting or rejecting what they hear. That's evangelism. And I believe that the evangelisation of the world is a necessary thing to take place before Jesus comes again. But whatever may be our views about the Second Coming there can be no difference of opinion that men without Christ are lost and ought to be reached with the Gospel. The last generation did not do it, the next generation may not do it. That puts a unique responsibility on this generation to do it, namely the evangelisation of the world now.

STOOPING TO CONQUER
(Philippians 2:5)

by the Revd. Canon Harry Sutton

William Barclay says that verses five to eleven of Philippians chapter two are in many ways the greatest and the most moving verses that Paul ever wrote about the Lord Jesus Christ. It may certainly be said that this passage of Scripture is unique for a number of different reasons. One of them being that in the gospels we have the history of the cross recorded and in the epistles we have the meaning of the cross explained. In this passage we are let into our Lord's mind concerning the cross. I want us to enter the mind of Christ, not out of spiritual curiosity, but that we might be enriched. That out of this entering into the mind of Christ there may be a new quality of living in the world on the part of every one of us.

When the Christian life is represented by this new quality in the world, I believe that unbelievers can more readily relate to the truth as it is in Jesus. Quite clearly, the proper nature of the Gospel is the way in which we tell others about Jesus. But when alongside what they hear they see the thing in action, then 'ear-gate' combining with 'eye-gate' enables them to understand the Gospel much more easily. So the purpose of our entering into the mind of Christ is that we may produce that mind in the quality of our own lives in the world today.

The letter to the Philippians is pre-eminently the letter of Christian experience. The revelation of the mind of Christ is given here in this passage in what some people have called 'The story of the great stoop'. We see Jesus in all his glory, and we see him coming down until at last he reaches the depths. The great stoop, the greatest act of his condescension was to be born. We will trace the steps of the great stoop and then we shall take a second step together. The first one is the *example of Christ*, and the second is the *exaltation of Christ*.

First, the example of Christ. 'Let his mind be in you which was also in Christ Jesus' (v. 5), and 'Who being in the form of God thought it not robbery to be equal with God' (v. 6). In verse six we see Jesus at the top of the ladder, the greatest stoop is about to begin. He is in the form of God – he did not play at being God, he was God, he is God. He has always been God and he always will be God. He was in the form of God. This phrase 'The form of God' means that Jesus has all the essential attributes of God. He was by very nature God, and Paul is saying here that Jesus was essentially, unalterably and unchangeably God. So we see him at the top of the ladder, as it were. I am not among those who see Jesus as just one great man among many great men, just one great religious leader, or even a super-charged Ghandi. Jesus is God, the Son of God. There is no one like Jesus, and there will be no one like him in the days that lie ahead. Now he begins to descend the ladder slowly, and in this descent we see our Lord as our own example in this life. Our Lord comes down from the throne, and we read

Stooping to Conquer

that he made himself of no reputation, and took upon himself the form of a servant. Not an easy verse to understand, verse seven, 'He emptied himself,' this deep humility. But whatever else this passage means it does not mean that our Lord emptied himself of deity. What it does mean is that he emptied himself of the glory that surrounds deity. It does not mean that he ever became anything less than majestic, but what it does mean is that he renounced the outward display of majesty. He remains throughout essentially God, but he divests himself of the glory of deity in this process of coming down, which we call the great stoop.

I believe that in this example Christ is saying to us that sometimes we need to step down from our homemade thrones. All too often we see ourselves in a too important light. So often we think that God could not do without us. I recall vividly going on holiday with my wife and family some years ago to Bournemouth, and I was very worried about the state of my parish. I telephoned my curate, but I couldn't contact him. However, the message got through to the secretary that the vicar wanted to know how things were in the parish. My secretary, who is a bit naughty, sent me a telegram. 'Vicar,' it said, 'you will be delighted to hear that in your absence God, together with a little help from your curate, is doing magnificently.' So often we see ourselves as a virtuoso in the service of God. But Jesus says, 'Come down from your throne.'

In verse seven, we read that 'He took upon himself the form of a slave' or of a servant. This word would be meaningful to the Philippians. For them, the idea of slavery meant that the one who was a slave lost everything in the world, liberty, freedom, will, possessions, even name. Everything was lost if you were a slave, so I don't believe that this word is here by accident, because this is precisely what the passage is trying to teach us. Those of us who would follow the Lord Jesus Christ in this twentieth century must experience something of the loss of a certain kind of liberty, freedom, will, possessions, and name if need be, in order that we may be his true slave in this world. Paul understood this perfectly when he wrote 'Not everyone of us lives for himself and not everyone does for himself for if we live we live for the Lord, or if we die, we die for the Lord, therefore, whether we live or die we are the Lord's.' (Romans 14:7–9). This captures the whole atmosphere of being his slave. Paul frequently refers to himself however as a 'Bond-slave of Jesus'. When we think of our salvation, we rightly think of the liberation that it brings, and of the many ways in which we have become uninhibited. There is a freeing, emancipating aspect of salvation, but there is also the opposite. There is a kind of loving, enslaving aspect to my relationship with Jesus. For instance, I am a slave to righteousness (Romans 6:18). And there are many such paradoxes in the Christian life. There is a form of captivity that is totally emancipating and makes me free, so that I can relax in the Lord. It also enables me to relate to other Christians in a perfectly lovely and meaningful way. Jesus said, 'If anyone wishes to come after me, let him deny himself.' Here we have the idea again. And so we see him now as he descends in the form of God – he empties himself, he humbles himself, he becomes a servant.

In the same verse we read that 'He was made in the likeness of men.' Just as Jesus did not play at being God, neither did he play at being man. He was man. He looked, acted and died as a man. He took to himself a new mode of living however, a mode of living which had

Stooping to Conquer

never been his before. 'His name shall be called Jesus.' He was given a human, common, everyday name. So this Lord Jesus Christ who was in the form of God is now in the form of man. It was not that he could not sin, but rather that he was tempted in all parts as we are and did not sin. He was made in the likeness of men and being fashioned as a man, 'He humbled himself and became obedient unto death, even the death on the cross.' It was his great delight to be the servant of all. Recently I read a new book on the history of the Salvation Army and I was thrilled to read of one Dr Samuel Logan Brindall. He was an American of great distinction, a scholar and great orator. When he left university he was offered one of the leading churches in the United States of America. Instead he came to Britain and offered his services to the Salvation Army, and was accepted as a probationary officer. His first job was to clean the shoes of the senior officers. But Dr Brindall said to himself, 'Are all my gifts to be dissipated in the cleaning of other people's shoes?' And these are his words, 'As I was thus reasoning in my mind, these words came to me, "He took a towel and girded himself."' With those words in mind, the polishing of shoes took on a sublime and spiritual significance. If the Master could take a towel and gird himself, how much more that great Dr Brindall. Christ in the great stoop comes as it were to the bottom of the ladder. In verse eight we read that 'He became obedient unto death, even the death of the cross.' Christian friends, I am so pleased that Jesus died. I don't just mean because through his death I am saved (though I do mean that too). I am glad Jesus was not translated in some sensational way and snatched off the cross in the last minute. I am glad that he went through the physical pangs of death, because he can share with me completely the great crises we call 'death'. He became obedient unto death, even the death of the cross.

We need to follow the example of his great stoop and discover that this display of the mind of Christ was progressive. It began with counting. 'He counted it not robbery to be equal with God,' and that counting led to self-abasement and in the end to self-oblation. There are many illustrations of this throughout the word of God. Take for instance just two, Moses and Paul. It is recorded of Moses (Hebrews 11:26) that he esteemed the reproach of Christ greater riches than the treasures in Egypt. Here was a counting process at work. Paul counted the very things in which he previously took the greatest pride as loss for the sake of Christ, 'I count all things but loss for the excellency of the knowledge of Christ.' So this counting process is one that leads on to self abasement and in the end to self oblation. The example of Christ. We see our Lord ascend back to Glory and here we see the exaltation of Christ. But it was God who highly exalted him and gave him a name that is above every name. There are at least three aspects of this responsive act of God as he sees the Lord Jesus. In verse nine, we see God responding, giving Jesus a glorious name. (Acts 4:12) I am finding it in my own Christian experience to be a saving name, each day I am finding the name of Jesus to be a salvation to me. Sometimes I feel unwell, with a spot of heart trouble, with frightening heart pains, when it's not easy to pray. But out of this feeling there comes the single name, the name of Jesus. It's a glorious name, a saving name, and also a soothing name. God responds to Jesus by making him the object of global worship (vv. 10a, 11a). We read that at the name of Jesus every knee

Stooping to Conquer

shall bow, every tongue confess. That is to say, every pagan tongue, every atheistic tongue, and even every blasphemer's tongue will confess that Jesus Christ is Lord. Your tongue and my tongue will confess that Jesus Christ is Lord. Some years ago, I sat round a fire in a little village in Northern Argentina, and talked with an old Indian who had once been a witch doctor. He told me that over thirty years ago he had heard the gospel, and was saved. It was an exciting moment. Within forty-eight hours I was on a jet plane flying over Peru. A Bolivian air hostess serving me said, 'Sir, I can tell from your appearance that you are a protestant pastor, and I would like you to know that I too am a believer in the Lord Jesus Christ.' She then asked me if she could talk with me after landing, adding, 'I don't get a lot of fellowship and I would like you to pray with me and for me.' And it came to me with fresh force that one day I was with a primitive Indian in Northern Argentina, a former witch doctor, and the next day I was with a sophisticated and attractive Bolivian air hostess. The two separated by two hundred years' social history. So what could unite them? They were united in the precious name of Jesus. They united in confessing Jesus as Lord, not because they had been beaten and broken into submission, but out of wonder, love and praise. And God responds by making Jesus the object of global worship.

In conclusion, God responds by making Jesus the means of glorifying the Father. When the Son is glorified, we glorify the Father. The honour of the Father, the Son and the Holy Spirit is inseparable. The aim of our Lord's life and ministry was to glorify the Father. Jesus draws men to himself and at the same time draws men to the Father. Here then is the mind of Christ.

Here is our pattern for Christian living in the world. He is our example, not only in his descent and humiliation, but also in his ascent and exaltation. And you may well ask how we follow this example. Is it by imitation? I've tried that and it's very difficult. I don't think the answer is to be found along those lines. If we are to possess the mind of Christ, and if the mind of Christ is to be demonstrated in us, and through us in the world, then I only know of one way. The reproduction of the mind of Christ in the life of the believer is supremely the work of God the Holy Spirit. It is as I submit to the Holy Spirit that he will work the miracle in me and the mind of Christ will be manifested in me. 'Be not conformed to this world, but be ye transformed by the renewing of your mind.' The work of that renewing is the work of God the Holy Spirit.

TWIN PERILS
Too Much – Too Little

by the Revd. Canon Harry Sutton

I want to present some thoughts arising from John 1:8, 9. 'If we say that we have no sin we deceive ourselves and the truth is not in us. If we confess our sins he is faithful and righteous to forgive us our sins and to cleanse us from all unrighteousness.' What we sometimes call the *Keswick Message* has lead to thousands all over the world being blessed. Some, however, have been perplexed. Perplexed because they hoped and prayed that as a result of some blessing, sin would go away. They had hoped, wrongly, that to be blessed by God in some special way inevitably meant that sin would leave them. And because after a day or two they discovered that this was not so, a sense of frustration began to appear in their Christian experience. The mistake that some of us make is to fail to distinguish between the *presence* of sin in the believer and the *power* of sin in the believer. Now the New Testament teaches very clearly that the presence of sin in the believer will remain until the Lord comes again. On the other hand the New Testament teaches with equal clarity, that the power of sin need not, and indeed should not, remain in the life of the believer. So that here we have the presence of sin, a reality all our lives, but the power of sin something that can and should be dealt with. While the presence of sin in the believer's life will, therefore, always be a reality, I believe that there is help at hand in order to overcome the power of sin in the nitty, gritty human situations of everyday life. Sin shall not have dominion over you. On the other hand, the Psalmist frequently cried out, 'My sin is ever before me.' With the Psalmist we recognise the presence of sin. But with the New Testament writer we look up to the Lord and we realise that although the presence of sin is a reality, the power of sin need not be and should not be in my life.

God's will for every one of us, I believe, is that we should live a victorious Christian life. If it is God's will that we should have a conflict experience, then it is also God's will that there should be victory in the conflict. The conflict experience of Paul (Romans 7) is one that ends in victory. Victory through Christ. And perfect faith will result in perfect victory. It is interesting to note that where the Psalmist speaks of the presence of sin in his life we do not have a general confession of sin. It's a very personalised sensitivity towards sin; my sin, my transgressions, my iniquities. He does not blame the circumstances. He does not blame the times in which he lived, nor does he blame his temperament, though I have no doubt but that all these things have a direct bearing on our inability to be victorious in the Christian life. Nevertheless the deed is the 'doers', and oftentimes with the Psalmist I am conscious that my sin is essentially my responsibility.

But what are these sins that so easily beset us today?

Twin Perils

In general terms, sin is rebellion against God. Sin is a missing of God's mark for us in the Christian life. But let us put the generalities on one side, and focus sharply on some of the sins that we as believers in the 20th Century have to cope with and over which, I believe, there is victory to be had now. I want to name one or two of the perils that beset us.

When preparing for this subject I asked some of my friends to share with me some of the areas in which they have special problems. And out of the sharing over several months two things became very clear. I see them as twin perils. *The peril of too much*, and *the peril of too little*. It is these twin perils that not only I find so difficult to deal with, but they are those of my friends.

The peril of too much in the life of the believer. Too much emphasis on 'things'. Christians, no less than others, are under constant pressure to join the mad scramble for more material possessions. Some will say that this is a fact of life in 1976, and we must adjust our thinking and habits to the times. It's quite true that God has not called us to be hermits, but I believe that he has called us to a new kind of living that puts 'things' second in our lives. The family that learns to live to a standard that it can really afford asks the question before buying a luxury article, 'Can we do without it?' Some Christians seem to regard the cross as a raft on which they, with their possessions, sail comfortably through life. In the March issue of the *Life of Faith*, Tim Dowry wrote an excellent article. He very courteously exhorted us to readjust our standard of living. In doing so he said, 'I want you to imagine the world as being condensed to one village of one hundred people, sixty-seven would be very poor, and thirty-three would be rich in varying degrees.' He went on to say that as this decade develops, the economic structures of the world are such that the sixty-seven will get poorer and the remainder will get richer. And now we as believers have to grapple with this problem. The peril of too much. There has never been a more propitious time for Christians to take seriously some modification in their life-style in order to consume less, waste less, and share more bountifully with others. I do not want Christians to wear hair shirts, nor to feel guilty about the world's problems. But I do suggest that the stewardship of our own resources should be constantly under review. I don't know who coined the phrase, but it's one that's used a lot nowadays, and it sums up what I am trying to say. 'God is calling us to live more simply in order that others may simply live.' If you are unconvinced that there is a case here then you might like to read James chapter five and Matthew chapter twenty-five verses thirty-one to forty-six. Such reorganisation of our living will be man's strong self-discipline. It's not just the reception of blessings but of our own discipline. If there's to be a reassessment of our life-style it will demand a very strong way of life. As the writer to Timothy says, 'God has not given us a timid spirit, but a spirit of power and love and discipline' (2 Tim. 1:7 Phillips). Every night one-third of the world goes to bed very hungry. You and I can help having readjusted our life-style. And let us then share what is left over with missionary societies or with TEAR Fund so that we may identify ourselves with those in need.

Then may I suggest that there may be too much time spent the wrong way. Since everyone seems to feel that time is money it seems harder and harder to find folks who'll give it. We notice this when we want to find a new church leader or a new Sunday school teacher.

Twin Perils

More and more of us take on more and more work in order to earn more and more money for bigger and better things at the cost of less and less time for the Lord and the Church. Now if this does not concern you so be it. I do not want you to feel a sense of guilt when it's not necessary. But for most of us I would suggest that there is a most urgent need today that we begin to live by priorities. I believe that there is room for recreation in our lives, for relaxation. Indeed some Christians need to spend more time relaxing and in re-creating. But for the majority of us I am not sure that this is so and I would invite you to consider this concept of too much time spent the wrong way. Oswald J. Saunders, in his excellent little book on *Discipleship*, opens up Ephesians (5:16) where we have the well known phrase 'Redeeming the time'. He says there are three steps that the average Christian can take in coping with the evil of too much time spent the wrong way. Stop the leaks in any given day. By that he means that if any part of the day is not being used to the best advantage, stop the leak, and use it to better advantage. Study priorities. So often we can be occupied with secondary things. Start planning. Try to find appropriate work. Not just work, we can all find that, but appropriate work for each day.

One other peril: too much reliance on the Generals to fight the war. By this I mean that we are still parson/pastor orientated when it comes to soul-winning. The average Christian opts out and leaves it to the pastor or the vicar, believing that the real war lies with the Generals and not with the troops. I believe that the real war lies with the troops as much as with the Generals and that we need to overcome the problem of too much reliance on the Generals. The Bishop of Winchester speaking about our response to God at last year's convention said, 'Where we serve the Lord, or the geography of our response, though very important, is of secondary importance. What is of primary importance is our availability to serve God where we are.' We don't have to go to Africa, India or South America, though I hope some of you will. Mission is where faith meets unfaith, where belief meets unbelief. On the tube, on the bus, anywhere at all. To this end, three years ago I asked the Lord to make me a true missionary. 'Lord,' I said, 'release me from being a professional missionary. I want to be a true missionary.' The next morning my car failed to go. So I believed it was the Lord saying to me, 'Right, you prayed last night for freedom to be a real witness. Now you've got it. Go on the tube this morning.' So I went down to the train. By the time the tube gets to Woodford Green it's always packed. But there was just one place vacant, and there were about three hundred people behind me, most of them ladies. So I said, 'This is the age of equality of the sexes, never mind them Harry, you get the seat there's a good boy.' So I got the seat. By the time we had all got in we were like sardines. And a little voice said to me, 'Now you have been saying that mission is wherever faith meets unfaith, the fellow sitting next to you is your mission field.' I looked at this fellow. He looked like death warmed up. So I said, 'Good morning, it's a lovely morning isn't it?' He said, 'Do you think so?' Oh, I said to myself, what a start. So I had another go with him. 'I had a great day yesterday, how did you get on?' 'Yesterday, Sunday!' I said. 'Yes, it was a great day.' 'A great day? What did you do?' 'Well as a matter of fact I met the living God three times.' 'You what!' he exclaimed. 'I met the living God three times,' I said. Well, the girl who was crushed up to me was reading *Annabel*.

Twin Perils

She rolled that up, put it under her arm and said, 'This is going to be better than anything in *Annabel*. This fellow's met the living God three times!' So we just talked about the living God, about Jesus. We have to fight the battle on the tubes, over the garden fence, on the bus, wherever faith meets unfaith.

We also have the peril of too little. I still believe that for the average Christian there is too little prayer. Year after year we quite rightly emphasise the urgent need of prayer, we applaud it but we very rarely get down to applying it. It's applied prayer that counts, not applauded prayer. I believe that these are days in which God is calling us to rediscover the exciting as well as the exhausting world of prayer. However, I would be a false friend if I gave the impression that all prayer is exciting. When I've met with the Lord and prevailed for the world I have felt as though everything has gone out of me. Mary Queen of Scots once said, 'I fear John Knox's prayers more than an army of 10,000 men.'

There is also too little Bible reading. Over the past fifty years among evangelicals there has been almost an obsession with what the theologians call 'homiletics'. But when the Bible has been rightly interpreted we have tended to put a stop there as though that was an end in itself. The understanding of the word of God is not an end in itself. The word of God is to be understood only to the end that it is applied. I am longing for the day when in our evangelical Bible study groups we study for half an hour instead of one hour. And with the other half hour we discuss how we are going to apply it in the world. How does this passage of Scripture apply to my relationship with my wife, and with my family, at work, at school, at play, in my recreation.

Finally, I believe that there is also too little reality

among us. All over Great Britain today I meet lovely Christian people who are reflecting the love of the Lord. However, there is a whole field of discovery in what I call 'reality'. So many of us are adept at wearing masks. I'm good at it myself. I have my clergyman's mask. A mask that I wouldn't dream of wearing in front of my wife. She'd say, 'Harry, I don't recognise you as the guy I married. Take it off.' We wear masks so that we never get to know the person in front of us. And if Christians don't ever get to know each other, how is the world ever going to get to know us? The only reason we wear masks is that we are afraid that if people saw us as we are they wouldn't like us. But does it matter? If Great Britain is not crying out, 'Sirs, what must I do to be saved?' that does not mean that she is not crying anything out. Great Britain is crying out, 'Are you Christians for real?' I believe that an increasing number of men and women are looking for reality. And seeing this reality of Jesus in our lives, they will then say, 'Sirs, what must I do to be saved, in order that I may share this reality with you?'

So I see Twin Perils – the peril on the one hand of *Too Much* and the peril on the other hand of *Too Little*. If in any measure you feel that way, as I often do, then there is good news for you. There is help at hand. God is willing and ready to share with us all the power that he has in order that we may be victorious in fighting these twin perils. But he will not bless us unless we want to be blessed.

THE DOUBLE REST
(Matthew 11:28, 29)

by the Revd. Dr. A. Skevington Wood

Two promises from the lips of Jesus: 'I will give you rest,' and 'You will find rest.' According to William Sanda, who taught at Oxford at the turn of the century, 'He who understands these words has found his way to the heart of Christianity.' They have to do with the Christian's relationship to Christ. The whole of the believer's life springs from his union with the Saviour, there is nothing that is not derived from Christ. In this passage our Lord speaks about what he offers to us in terms of rest. The word really means refreshment or reinvigoration. A rest from our own feverish yet futile activism, and a total reliance on him for all that we need.

By picking out two salient phrases in a more extended saying of Jesus, I have deliberately drawn attention to the fact that a double rest is involved. This is not only the same rest looked at from two different angles, his and ours, there is also an immediate rest and a continuing rest. There is the rest that is bestowed on all who come to Christ and commit themselves to Him. And there is the rest experienced by those who are prepared to take his yoke upon them. Both are altogether in Christ and cannot be had apart from him. They belong to successive stages of the Christian life since one is intended to run into the other. The one is the rest that is given to those who put their trust in the Saviour as they come out of their bondage, sorrow and night. The other is the rest that is found by those who are going on with Christ and discover that only perfect submission brings perfect delight.

First, this double rest is described both as a gift and discovery. Originally rest is entered into simply by coming to Christ. It is independent of any conditions except repentance and faith. It is a gift of grace. Our Lord lifts the burden of transgression from our shoulders and carries it himself. This is the rest received by all who turn to Christ, it may be theirs without delay and in ample measure. All Christians have once known this rest for they could not otherwise have become Christians. Not all Christians, however, are claiming it and realising it now. This is because it can only be retained when the conditions governing its offer have been met. It is still a gift of grace, but also a discovery reserved for those who enlist in the school of Christ. There is no admission to the classroom at all until the initial rest has been received, but equally there is no entrance into the further rest until the training course has begun.

Consider another feature of Christ's teaching on this theme. This double rest is expressed both by a verb and a noun. 'I will give you rest' or, literally, *I will rest you*, and 'You will find rest.' That would appear to mean that rest is a maintained condition. In other words, having received such rest the Christian is meant to enjoy it as a permanent possession. An up and down sort of existence

The Double Rest

is not the ideal which the New Testament sets before us. Instead we are offered the prospect of an uninterrupted resting in the Lord. However busy or pressurised, however assailed by Satan, we may nevertheless abide under the shadow of the Almighty. This double rest is a blessing for the pure in heart. Its nature can be illustrated from the history of God's people under the old covenant, after the Israelites escaped from Egypt. When they had covered many miles over land and crossed the sea to the further bank, they paused to rest. They looked back and saw the Egyptians dead on the seashore, and recognised that it was all the work of the Lord. They feared God and believed in him. They joined in the song of victory. That was their initial rest before they pressed on across the desert. That is the rest the believer enjoys after he has been delivered from the bondage of Satan and tasted the salvation of God.

But a further rest lay in store for the children of Israel. The promised land was their inheritance. There came a day, delayed by their disobedience, when they crossed over into Canaan. They exchanged a nomadic life for a permanent residence. We are told that the Lord provided a place of rest as he had promised. This is like the double rest which Jesus offers and each Christian may claim it now. There is Canaan below as well as Canaan above. By virtue of our union with Christ our privilege is already to be seated with him in the heavenly places.

Consider the final factor in Christ's teaching in this passage. This double rest is urged both through an invitation and a command. Rest is given in response to an invitation. *Come.* But once we have yielded to Christ, his word is an absolute command. The command through which believers are urged to find Christ's rest is twofold. *Take* and *learn*. 'Take my Yoke upon you and learn from me.' If Christians are to be effective in work and witness they must come under the yoke. That involves the abandonment of our own will and the acceptance of God's will. The hardest thing to do is to give up the control of our own lives, yet this is what union with Christ means. The yoke of Christ is different. It is not irksome but light. It is not meant to be a burden but it makes for rest. We are not only to learn about him, he is to be our personal tutor. It is our relationship with him that matters. We are to be scholars in his school, and if that should strike at our pride we are immediately reminded that he himself is meek and lowly in heart. He learned obedience through the things that he suffered, and that is his way of teaching us. For our union with Christ is in the fellowship of his sufferings. We can never know the rest he offers while a scrap of self-concern remains.

If we would know the revitalising power of his resurrection we must not shrink from the fellowship of his sufferings. It is at the cross that self is slain that Christ may reign. It is there that we find the rest that he undertakes to give.

THE COMFORTER
(John 14:16)

by the Revd. Dr. A. Skevington Wood

'And I will pray the Father and he shall give you another comforter that he may abide with you forever.' Jesus enheartened his disciples with this remarkable assurance whilst he was still with them in the flesh, and it was put into effect after the ascension when he returned to the place of authority at his Father's right hand where he began his unique ministry of heavenly intercession on behalf of those who were his own. His first request was that the Holy Spirit should be bestowed. And in verse seventeen the identity of the Comforter is revealed. He is the 'Spirit of truth'. The world is incapable of receiving him, let alone realising his presence in personal experience, but the disciples of Jesus already knew him and would soon be aware of his indwelling in a special way. The Father had promised, the Son prayed, and the Spirit was poured out, that was how Pentecost happened.

It is noticeable in reviewing the teaching of Jesus that comparatively little was revealed about the Holy Spirit during his active ministry. There was no need for that, his deeds were sufficiently eloquent. To all who had eyes to see it was plain that the Spirit was all the time at work in our Lord, and his very words, though not often about the Spirit, were all in the Spirit and from the Spirit. The descent of the Spirit at his baptism in the outward form of a dove symbolised the continuing endowment of his entire ministry. All the fullness of the Spirit was his without any restriction as John the Baptiser testified, 'God did not give his Spirit by measure to our Lord, all the plenitude of the Spirit's power was manifested in the incarnate Son.'

It was only as the end approached and Jesus faced the bitter cross that he found it necessary to tell his disciples more about the Holy Spirit as the Holy Spirit concerned them. Now that the Master was to go from his men they must be informed about the gift that was to be made over to them when he ascended to glory. Here in the gospel of John the many references to the Spirit (chs. 14–16) are placed in the context of the upper room before the Saviour went out to his agony and arrest in the garden of Gethsemane. The discourse recorded here begins as Jesus explains his departure. The disciples are dismayed to realise that he is about to leave them. Thomas voices the feelings of the rest as he takes exception to the statement of the Lord that they already know where he is going. Of course, they should have known for Jesus had been preparing them for it all along. But as yet they were unable to grasp the fact that soon they would no longer enjoy his physical presence. What he had to tell them about the place he intended to prepare for them, and how he would come again to take them there, was largely lost on them because of their preoccupation with their immediate plight. It is then, in the midst of their distress at the prospect of his

The Comforter

departure, that our Lord reassures his disciples that they will not be left like orphans to shift for themselves. He has made better provisions for them. He will ensure that the Comforter is sent to make his presence real to them still and to strengthen them for all that they are called upon to do in his name. Let us then discover what this verse has to teach us about the Holy Spirit in the particular role that is assigned to him here, as there is an especial need in these days of a clear understanding from the word of God what his ministry is.

We learn in the first place that the Holy Spirit is a Comforter. That is one of many titles accorded him in Scripture. It is perhaps the best known but in some ways the least understood. The word 'comforter' in English rather tends to suggest that the primary function of the third person of the Trinity is to console or even to cosset; to us comfort spells either solace and soothing, or cushioned and carpet-slippered ease – but that is not what is intended here. When the AV was produced Comforter was a perfectly good rendering, but since then the impact of this word has been softened. By derivation it meant not to pamper but to support. It stems from the Latin 'confortis', 'with strength'. The Holy Spirit is sent to equip us with power, he is the enabler. The Greek word in the New Testament is 'paracletos', literally this means one called on to be alongside us. Imagine a man in a state of collapse, his knees sagging and about to fall in a heap, then someone comes alongside him, holds him up and stands him on his feet again. That is what it means to be a paraclete, a comforter. The same word describes one who is called in to be alongside a defendant in a court of law, an expert adviser or an advocate, which is why some translations have counsellor. Nevertheless the basic implication of the term is that of a strengthener or helper whatever the need may be. In all the trying circumstances of life the Holy Spirit stands by ready to step in whenever our resources fail. And, of course, apart from him our resources will always fail, that is why we have to seek his aid all the time. There is an everyday expression which exactly answers to the ministry of the Holy Spirit as Comforter. When we have had one of those days in which everything seems to have gone wrong we reach the end of our tether. The Holy Spirit is the one who copes for us as Christians. When we realise and confess that we are unable to handle the situation ourselves we can appeal to him, and he will come and cope for us.

However the Spirit does more than enable us to meet the pressures of life as they threaten to get us down. It is also part of his work as Comforter to spur us on to do battle against Satan and sin, and to share in Christ's conquest over all the forces of evil. The Christian is engaged in spiritual warfare. He fights on two fronts. He is continually assailed within himself by the running contest between flesh and spirit, that is between our lower nature, which, as Paul tells the Galatians, sets its desires against the spirit, and the Holy Spirit who fights against it. But in his ministry as Comforter the Spirit ensures that the believer gains the victory. The Christian is also involved in the conflict with sin in the world around him as he is identified with Christ's redemptive mission. The more effective he seeks to be as a witness and a contender for the fight, the more likely he is to receive the brunt of Satan's attack. Here, too, in the thick of the battle when the flame tipped arrows of the enemy are flying fast the Holy Spirit gives him courage and strength, and if he should be at all reluctant the same

The Comforter

Spirit will urge him on. One of the scenes depicted on the Bayeux tapestry shows William the Conqueror marching behind his troops with a drawn sword in his hand, evidently prodding them on to deeds of valour, and beneath is this legend, 'King William comforteth his soldiers'. That is the precise meaning of the word as it was originally used and that is what the Holy Spirit does as Comforter. He pushes us forward inciting us to be strong and to do exploits for God.

But Jesus here not only speaks of a Comforter, he speaks of 'another' Comforter, implying that there was already a Comforter. And this is Jesus himself. He was always there alongside to help his men, to counsel, encourage and inspire. From the moment he called the twelve he was their Comforter. They could cope when he was there. In his absence, as on the Mount of Transfiguration, they were sadly ineffective. Between his death on the cross and the coming of the Spirit at Pentecost, they were altogether helpless. But he had already assured them that when his bodily presence was withdrawn he would ask the Father to send them another Comforter to be to them what he himself had been and even more. Jesus had been *with* them, this other Comforter would be more than with them, he would be *in* them.

There are two words in Greek for 'another'. One means 'Of a *different* kind', the other means 'Another of the *same* kind'. That is the word Jesus uses when he speaks about the Holy Spirit as another Comforter, a Comforter of exactly the same kind as Jesus had been to the disciples. They turned to him whenever they needed him and he was there. So is the Holy Spirit, the Comforter. The 'Paraclete' then fulfills the role of Jesus at the side of his followers, or to put it in another way, he enables them to realise the living presence of Christ. That is why it can be rightly said that Pentecost made Easter permanently real for the disciples. It was only in the Spirit that they experienced the power of the risen Christ. Look at some verses in these chapters which suggest how the Spirit acts as another Comforter, doing what Christ himself had done and being what he had been. Begin with chapter fourteen verse twenty-six, 'He shall teach you all things.' Jesus was their teacher, the Holy Spirit, the Spirit of truth is our teacher now. Go on to verse twenty-six of chapter fifteen, 'He shall testify of me.' Jesus was real to his disciples when he was incarnate, the Holy Spirit makes him real still. Finally, 'He will guide you into all truth ... he will show you things to come' (16:13). Jesus in the days of his flesh was their guide, now the Holy Spirit is our guide, he leads us through the present and opens up the future. Yet all this is not an either/or. It is a both, the Spirit is the Spirit of Christ. He comes not to be a substitute for Christ's absence, but to complete his presence. Hence our Lord could summarise the ministry of the Spirit in the significant disclosure, 'He shall glorify me' (16:14).

However Jesus not only speaks here of a Comforter and another Comforter, but of an *abiding* Comforter. In the Old Testament dispensation, the Spirit's presence was intermittent, he visited certain men to equip them for certain tasks. But at Pentecost the Spirit was no transient phenomenon, he was poured out as a permanent enablement. The tongues 'Like flames of fire' were distributed to all and remained on each. The Spirit came to abide forever with the Church and with the believer. The Christian today does not need to plead that the Spirit may be given, he rejoices that the Spirit has been given, and he seeks to realise the repercussions of such a bestowal in his own experience and witness. The word 'forever' denotes time without limit. The Holy Spirit is a gift for eternity. The Spirit-filled believer may remain filled with the Spirit moment by moment until moments are no more and then into endless ages. That is why what took place at Pentecost is in one sense unique and yet in another sense can always be renewed. It is unique in that there can never be another initial effusion of the Spirit to produce the Church. It can always be renewer however, in the sense that what happened at Pentecost can happen still.

'With us,' and more than that, 'He . . . shall be in you.' Not only *with*, but *in*. God could assure Moses, 'My presence shall go with you.' He could promise in Isaiah, 'When thou passeth through the waters I will be with thee.' The ascended Christ said, 'Lo I am with you always.' Since Pentecost, however, Scripture can speak of *in*, as well as *with*. 'Know ye not that ye are the Temple of God,' Paul asked the Corinthians, 'and that the Spirit of God dwelleth in you,' 'Whosoever shall confess that Jesus is the Son of God,' announces John, 'God dwelleth in him and he in God.' 'Christ in you is the hope of Glory,' so Paul informs the Colossians. The Spirit of Christ, the Spirit of Glory and of God abides not only with, but in.

The crucial question with which we must close must be this: does the Spirit indeed abide in us, are we always drawing on the inner resources his dwelling provides, is the fruit of the Spirit our unending source of strength and adequacy? Or do we have to admit that we have been leading a sub-normal Christian life, grovelling in the valley of indifference if not of defeat, when we could be and should be on the victory side? The uplands of the Spirit are accessible to us as we confess our shameful failure and loss. That is the only condition of restoration. To get back to Pentecost we need to return to the cross, as we lie broken there in utter humiliation and genuine repentance, and God will prove himself yet again as good as his Word in enabling us to realise the availability of another Comforter to abide with us forever. The promise of Jesus first given to the twelve is extended to include us too, 'I will pray the Father and he will give you another Comforter, that he may abide with you forever.'

It was while staying with Paul Kruger on his farm in the Transvaal that Andrew Murray entered into the fullness of this experience. Here is how he wrote about it to his wife: 'The thought of the blessing of the indwelling Spirit appears so clear the prospect of being filled with him at moments so near, that I could almost feel sure that we would yet attain this happiness. The wretchedness of the uncertain life we mostly lead, the certainty that it cannot be the Lord's pleasure to withhold from his bride the full communion of his love, the glorious prospect of what we can be and do if truly filled with the Spirit of God, all this combines to force one to be bold with God and say, "I will not let thee go except thou bless me".' This is our inheritance as Christians, to be filled with the Holy Ghost the Comforter.

KESWICK CONVENTION TAPE LIBRARY

Tape recordings are available on both reels and cassettes of most recent Convention addresses, together with a selection from earlier Conventions. All Bible Readings are stocked from 1957, and the recordings of the Centenary Convention addresses in 1975 are especially recommended.

Recordings may be obtained on loan for a period of ONE MONTH for a suitable donation, and on permanent loan for a donation as indicated on the official order form.

Details of ALL Library Lists, Honorary Tape Librarians abroad, order forms, etc., may be obtained from:

**Anthony C. Gill, Tape Secretary,
Keswick Convention Tape Library,
13 Lismore Road,
EASTBOURNE, E. Sussex.
BN21 3BA, England.**

Tel: Eastbourne (0323) 25938.

1976 TAPE LIST

No.	Title	Speaker
480	'He blessed him there'	Revd. George B. Duncan

BIBLE READINGS –
'The Fellowship of Light and Love.'
(First Epistle of John) .. .. Revd. Eric Alexander

No.	Title	
481	The Message and its Implications (1:1–2:2)	
482	The Evidence of Walking in the Light (2:3–2:29)	
483	The Privileges and Obligations of being Children of God (3:1–4:6)	
484	The Implications of Abiding in Love (4:7–5:12) and Conclusion: The Full Assurance of Faith (5:13–21)	
485	OVERSEAS BROADCAST SERVICE	Revd. Eric Alexander
486	A Leader to Love	Revd. Tom Houston
487	The Keswick Message To-day	Bishop Maurice Wood
488	The Way of Renewal	Revd. Alan Redpath
489	Release from our Past	Revd. Tom Houston
490	Christians Under Pressure	Revd. Gordon Bridger
491	Living in the Light of His Return	Revd. Alan Redpath
492	The Comforter (John 14:16)	Dr. A. Skevington Wood
493	**General Missionary Meeting**	Mr. E. W. Oliver
494	**MINISTERS' MEETING**	Revd. George B. Duncan
495	Twin Perils: – Too Much – Too Little	Canon Harry Sutton
496	Stooping to Conquer	Canon Harry Sutton
497	Servants of the King	Canon Harry Sutton
498	Freedom of the Spirit	Canon Harry Sutton
499	Peter Was to be Blamed (Gal. 2:1–21)	Revd. Derek Prime
500	The Weakness of Strength	Revd. Alan Redpath
501	The Double Rest (Matt. 11:28, 29)	Dr. A. Skevington Wood
502	The Lifting-up of the Downcast	Revd. Eric Alexander
503	'You call me Lord'	Revd. Gordon Bridger
504	A Threefold Test of Discipleship	Revd. George B. Duncan
505	The Liberating Spirit (Rom. 7:21–8:17)	Revd. G. Osei-Mensah
506	The Freedom We Need	Revd. Tom Houston

No.	Title	Speaker
510	An Answered Prayer	Revd. Gilbert W. Kirby

BIBLE READINGS –
'A Single, Steady Aim.' (Nehemiah).. Revd. Alec. Motyer

511	Beginning: Getting the Foundations Right (1:1–3:32)	
512	Persevering: Stress-points and Strong Points (4:1–6:19)	
513	Living: a. The Citizen's Charter (7:1–9:38)	
514	Living: b. The Enemy Within (10:1–13:31)	
515	The Fullness of Grace (Jn. 1:14–18)	Revd. Michael Cole
516	Our Covenant-keeping God (Heb. 6:13–20 & Heb. 10)	Revd. G. Osei-Mensah
517	God's Searching Questions (Gen. 3:1–15)	Revd. G. Osei-Mensah
518	I Saw the Lord (Isa. 6:1–7)..	Revd. Michael Cole
519	Prelude to Victory (Mk. 14:32–42)	Mr. Alan Nute
520	The Secret of Peace ..	Revd. Gilbert W. Kirby
521	Christ in the Heart (1 Peter 3:13–16)	Revd. Gervais Angel
522	A Living Sacrifice (Romans 12)	Revd. G. Osei-Mensah
523	The Spirit of Sonship (Rom. 8:14–17)	Mr. Alan Nute
524	The Comfort of the Holy Spirit	Revd. Alec Motyer

SERVICE AND OUTREACH MEETING –

525	Called to Serve	Revd. Gilbert W. Kirby

We hope you have benefited
by reading

KESWICK SEVENTYSIX

Why not purchase extra copies
as worthwhile gifts for your
friends?

*Obtainable from your
usual bookseller.*

In case of difficulty write
to:–

**Coverdale House Publishers,
Lottbridge Drove, Eastbourne,
East Sussex BN23 6NT**